Gaits of Gold:
Selecting, Fitting, and Training
the Naturally Gaited Horse

Other titles by Brenda Imus:

From the Ground Up: Horsemanship for the Adult Rider
Heavenly Gaits: The Complete Guide to Gaited Riding Horses
Leah's Song: A Novel

Books distributed by CrossOver Publications
may be ordered toll-free by calling 888-617-8009

ISBN: 0-9648366-7-X

Gaits of Gold

Selecting, Fitting, and Training the Naturally Gaited Horse

By Brenda Imus
Photos by Mickey Anderson
Illustrations by Brita Barlow Eadie

CrossOver Publications, New York

Cover Art based on photo by Mickey Anderson
Stallion: Time Slips Away, Fallen Timber Farm
Clif Johnson up

To the Lord Jesus Christ,
who walks me beside still waters.

Table of Contents

Foreword

Talk to two genuinely experienced, knowledgeable horsemen on any single horse-related subject and you'll almost certainly get two different opinions and points of view. If you ever discover two horsemen who think alike on everything pertaining to horses, you've likely discovered the results of the first secret human cloning experiment!

So I don't expect all of the readers of this book to agree with the thoughts and methods put forth here. Nevertheless, I believe this book will offer the everyday amateur horse lover some useful, safe and much-needed advice on how to bring out the best in a horse with intermediate saddle gaits (a 'gaited' horse). The state of the gaited horse industry in general makes this a worthwhile goal.

The industry is growing by leaps and bounds and, except for a few little-known, hard-to-find breed-specific books, there is little reliable information out there about training naturally gaited horses. Many of the books that are available assume a degree of horsemanship sophistication that may well be beyond the skills of the average owner/rider. Others suggest using training methods and devices that are for the most part unnecessary, and often downright inhumane.

Gaits of Gold

Most of us don't want to become expert horse trainers, even if that were possible. We simply want to be able to bring out the best in our own horses, to make them more enjoyable to ride. This is a goal well within the reach of most horse owners. **Gaits of Gold** is geared toward those of you who simply want to turn out a horse that is willing, smooth, and fun to ride–without having to take out a second mortgage to pay the trainer's bill.

This might seem to be a fairly simple task, but the history and background of gaited horses overall complicates the picture. Many of these horses come from gene pools that have been created by breeding horses that possess traits useful only to the artificial horse show industry. The results of this are Tennessee Walking Horses who are high-headed, nervous and extremely pacey, Missouri Fox Trotters who stumble over flat dirt, and Paso Finos with exaggeratedly short strides who wear out too young and are of limited practical use. Too often, when these horses prove to be unsatisfactory riding mounts, the owners decide to use them for breeding instead, thus exacerbating the problems.

Further complicating matters, the sudden popularity of gaited riding horses has created a demand that exceeds supply. This invites unscrupulous and careless breeders in on the act, and causes otherwise nice folks to act in an unreasonable fashion when it comes to registering and promoting their horses.

Just this week I received a call from a Canadian horse trainer who is working with a young stallion, not yet two years old. This animal's gaited breed association rules declare that horses being considered for registration must be shown gaiting, *under saddle*, by their two-year-old birthday. The horse she was working with wouldn't cooperate–and who could blame him? The trainer was convinced that the horse was far too immature to be training under saddle, let alone gaiting at speed. All I could do was agree with her, and promise to send a letter off to the breed association urging them to adopt more reasonable, humane rules. I don't have much faith that it will do any good, since in essence this horse–and every one like it–is being placed on the breed association's production line. Like all money-making enterprises, they're eager to turn out product–too often at the expense of quality.

To my sorrow, I've observed this phenomenon among several breed associations, and the owners are pleased to cooperate with 'market demands.' They begin breeding for exaggerated color, or try to do in one or two generations what can only be well-integrated in six, or ten. Unwary buyers go to these breeders/dealers and end up with young horses that will never gait properly, adjust to the environment of real world use, or hold up well physically under normal riding conditions.

There are few books or study aids out there that can help the gaited horse enthusiast avoid these problems, or deal with them when or if they crop up. My first book, **Heavenly Gaits**, made inroads in this area. It gave an overview of gaited horses in general, and each breed in particular. But one book can only accomplish so much, and since the publication of **Heavenly Gaits**, I've been inundated with requests from people who want more training-specific information for gaited horses. I'm honored at their faith in me, and this book is my attempt to fill that gap.

Every gaited breed is gleefully touted as 'naturally gaited.' Yet the unwary buyer too often discovers that--even if the horse does possess a natural intermediate saddle gait–it needs to be reinforced through training. Too often, the gait which the horse is supposed to perform isn't genetically well-fixed at all, and the rider needs to determine if it would be better to shift gears to another gait–or horse–altogether. Even when all things are optimum with the horse, it may be that the rider simply doesn't know what the various gaits are, how to tell them apart, or how to ride them very well.

All of these factors may negate the very real benefits of owning and riding a gaited horse, and turn other horse people off from these wonderful animals.

And so, with no small amount of trepidation, I'm going to try to address some of these issues for the benefit of both the gaited horse, and the interested horse person. It seems that everyone has a different idea about how I should approach this topic. Some insist that I should include information regarding mechanical training 'shortcuts' that can be used to assist gait. Still others are certain that the only way to do the job right is by teaching people how to use high level dressage methods on their animals so that within three or four years they will have produced truly finished riding horses. Yet another camp doesn't believe this job can be done by amateur owner/riders at all, but should be left strictly to the professional trainer.

I disagree with all of these approaches. It is my contention that there is no room for mechanical shortcuts in the training of horses. If the horse won't perform the desired gait using natural means, then it is inhumane—and ultimately self-defeating—to use mechanical means to that end. I also believe that people don't want or need a long treatise on the theories of 'high school' dressage, but an understandable, practical guide that will allow them to measure progress by the hour and the day, rather than by the year.

As for the average person being unable to train the average horse—poppycock! I never owned my own horse until I was in my mid-thirties. Scarcely a dozen years later I've successfully ridden and trained a number of them myself, gaited and otherwise. Let me hasten to add that I do not consider myself an especially gifted horse person. If I can do it, so can you!

I've adapted what I've learned from research and personal experience to try to produce a book that is easy to understand and extraordinarily easy and practical in its application. What's more, those who apply themselves to working to bring out the **best** in their gaited riding horses by using these methods are going to have fun in the process. They're going to get to know themselves, and their horses, at least a little better than they did before.

Isn't that what owning a horse should be all about?

Introduction

People have a tendency to make things complicated. This is as true of horse training as anything else. It seems like some mysterious science, far beyond our talents or capabilities. So we trust the work to 'professionals,' people who run horses through their training barns the way factories run parts through the assembly line.

Trouble is, all too often that's the way horses are treated at such facilities: as commodities, one identical to the next. Of course, nothing could be further from the truth. Regardless of this fact, the trainer only gets paid for an acceptable 'product,' and the work has to be done in quick time besides. So the temptation is to use gimmicks and shortcuts, methods that will get the job done, no matter the long-term damage to the animal, physically and mentally.

I'm well aware this isn't true at **all** training barns. There are sensitive, ethical horse trainers out there. However, such services aren't cheap. The time that the horse spends at the trainer's barn—considerable, for a good job—means time that it's not spending with you, the owner and rider. No matter how good the training, ultimately it is the rider who must learn how to bring out and maintain the best manners and gaits of the horse. Since this is the case, why not simply start out by doing the job yourself?

A note of caution: though most riders are capable of training their horse to perform good saddle gaits, and to be mannerly, there are some situations that should be avoided for safety's sake. If you've somehow come into ownership of a horse that is spoiled and insists on indulging in unsafe practices, then by all means get yourself and the horse into the hands of a professional horse trainer. Unless you are an extremely experienced and competent rider, you should never try to train a horse that habitually rears, bucks hard, or balks strenuously in any way. The lessons in this book may be helpful for horses that have a mild balking problem, but retraining a truly spoiled horse is no job for amateurs. I don't want to unwittingly encourage anyone in that regard.

A young horse totally untrained to saddle also needs to be started by an experienced rider. If you're inexperienced, or lack confidence for this kind of work, then my advice is to use a professional trainer to get the horse properly started, or depend on the help of a more experienced friend. You might also consider investing in a few riding lessons, to learn correct cues and balance. Work closely with your trainer to get to know your horse during the early days of its training, and establish a firm foundation of trust that can be built upon as you take its training beyond the elementary level.

Having explained the exceptions to the 'owner can train' rule, let's get on with talking about gaited horses, shall we?

Note: For those who feel they lack enough basic horsemanship knowledge to undertake the tasks in this book, may I suggest either—or both—of my previous two equestrian titles? The first, **From the Ground Up: Horsemanship for the Adult Rider**, will give the adult novice horse lover some very useful tools and information to help increase knowledge, ability and confidence. The second, **Heavenly Gaits: The Complete Guide to Gaited**

Riding Horses, should be prerequisite reading for anyone desiring to own or train any type of gaited horse.

Order information for these titles may be found at the front of this book.

Acknowledgments

Many people contributed to the publication of this book. As with most ambitious endeavors, for awhile it seemed like anything that could go wrong *did* go wrong. But it all came together at last with the help of a few key people. I owe a real debt of gratitude to Mickey Anderson for the excellent photographs she supplied, on very short notice. Also deserving special appreciation are Clif Johnson and Diane Deist of Fallen Timber Farm, and Chris and John McKinney of Echoing Hills Farm. These folks went the extra mile to accommodate Mickey's requests for human and equestrian models. Jean Blackman and her special stallion, Go Boy's Merry Chance B, (featured on last page of chapter 7) should be an inspiration to us all.

Brita Barlow Eadie (no relationship to Mr. Eldon Eadie), provided all of the line drawings I requested to help make each lesson clear. She did so on top of a work load that would cause most people to lay down and quit trying!

Audrey Reed is an accomplished writer and gaited horse person in her own right. When she heard of my plans to write this book, she sent me a huge box filled with what must surely have been every gaited horse magazine ever published. What an incredibly rare and rich resource! Thank you, Audrey, for that generous gesture.

I couldn't have finished this work at all if my husband Hugh hadn't picked up the slack around our home and farm for several long weeks. Not only did he do more than his share of mucking out both house and barn, but got so he could prepare a pretty mean chicken casserole as well! Hugh—you're the best.

Most of all I want to thank you, my readers, for inspiring me to take on this task. It was both a personal and professional challenge to sort out and make sense of all the information, and *mis*information, that is available regarding gaited horses. Everything had to be checked, double-checked, and often tested personally. I was painfully aware that there are few written standards for these types of horses, so what I chose to publish could affect them for good or otherwise for a long time to come. This responsibility—combined with the knowledge that no matter what I wrote some people would vigorously disagree with it—tended to weigh me down. Complicating matters, on several occasions things just seemed to fall apart. Computers and software programs crashed at critical times, production schedules went awry, and so on and so forth. This year the unusually warm weather we had in upstate New York tried hard to lure me away from my desk and into the saddle. For a variety of reasons, I was tempted more than once to go on to other things and let someone else take up this task. But then I'd remember those of you who would be disappointed, and take a deep breath and get back to it. It was your trust and high expectations that kept me going.

Many thanks to all of you for keeping the fire lit. I trust this book will be of value to you—and to your very special horses.

*Much of what follows in this chapter was borrowed directly from my first book, **Heavenly Gaits**. After struggling for several days to write it differently, I finally decided: Why fix what's not broken?*

Chapter One
The Gaits of a Horse

What is Gait?

All vertebrates, including man, may be said to have gaits. We can run, jog and walk. In addition, we may two-step, skip, and perform dance steps such as the rhumba or waltz. These are all different gaits. Each person has an individual way or style of performing these gaits. Besides this, we may perform them differently at various times. We may, in our own individual style, walk energetically forward, walk with a spring to our step, walk stiff-legged, walk as though marching, walk dispiritedly, drag our feet— the list goes on. Likewise we can perform our other gaits in varying ways. If all of this makes it seem like we two-legged humans possess an almost infinite repertoire of movement, imagine how much greater that repertoire would be if we, like the horse, possessed four legs rather than two!

The horse's gait may be described as his manner of moving especially, but not exclusively, as it relates to the order of footfalls. Strictly speaking, all horses are gaited insofar as they all have some manner of moving across the ground.

Gaits of Gold

The term 'gaited horse' has commonly come to mean horses that boast gaits other than the walk, trot and canter. These are the three most common–or at least most well-known–gaits. Even more specifically, it refers to horses that use gaits alternate to the trot. These are referred to as intermediate gaits.

Because the horse possesses so many possible gaits, we need to break this subject into understandable components. The most common way this is done is to categorize most of the horse's gaits as either lateral or diagonal. That is, either the horse moves same-side (lateral) sets of legs in unison, or it moves diagonally opposed sets of legs in unison. To understand what constitutes a lateral or diagonal gait is to begin understanding what a gait really is.

The Two Perfect Lateral/Diagonal Gaits

The Pace

Lateral gaits are those where the horse's same side fore and hind legs move forward together; i.e.: left fore and hind, right fore and hind.

The purest example of a lateral gait is the pace, where the same side fore and hind legs move in synchrony and the lateral sets of feet land in perfect unison. The pace is a two-beat gait; that is, since the fore and hind feet on each side land at the same time, the two feet produce a single "beat" of sound. Also, there is a moment of suspension between the time the legs on one side lift from the ground and the legs of the opposite side set down. This creates a discernible space or unit of time between each beat. So the pace sounds like 1–2; 1–2.

The Trot

Diagonal gaits are those in which the horse's legs at opposite corners, or diagonally opposed limbs, move forward in unison; i.e.: left hind and right fore; right hind and left fore.

The purest diagonal gait is the trot, where diagonal sets of legs move forward precisely together and the feet strike the ground in perfect unison. Like the pace, the trot is also a two-beat gait with a moment of suspension, or discernible space, making it sound like 1–2; 1–2.

The Pace

The Trot

What Determines Gait?

The timing of the hind legs as they relate to the motion of the forelegs determines whether a gait is lateral or diagonal. If the horse synchronizes same-side hind and fore legs, as in the pace, then the gait is lateral. If same-side fore and hind legs move in opposition to one another, as in the trot, the gait is diagonal. The changing relationship between hind and fore legs all along the spectrum between these two extremes is what creates the gaits unique to the gaited riding horse.

Not all horses are capable of fast lateral motion such as the pace. These horses–which in our generation constitute the majority–are strictly trotters. Those that can pace, or at least move their hind legs somewhat out-of-synch with the true diagonal trot, are capable of producing one or more of the specialized gaits. The more ability of motion the horse has along this spectrum, the greater his range of gait.

The Walk

If you've ever casually observed a horse walking across a field and tried to ascertain the order of footfalls, you were likely frustrated in your endeavor due to the difficulty of keeping track of all those legs moving independently. One moment it may have appeared that the horse's hind leg contacted the ground just ahead of the same side fore–but then, no!–surely it was the fore foot that landed just before the opposite side hind. Just when did that front foot come off the ground, anyway? Somehow you missed something–better try again. Chances are, unless you were extremely determined, you quit trying to analyze the horse's walk.

But it's not hard to understand the walk once you learn how to look at it. The order of footfalls for the walk is: left hind, left front; right hind, right front. Simple, right? The walking gait only becomes confusing when you lose track of a leg and then begin observing the horse's walk at a point in the footfall sequence when a fore, rather than a hind, foot contacts the ground. Then the gait appears to be diagonal, and looks like this: left front, right hind; right front, left hind.

The timing of the footfalls in a good flat walk is even, so that each foot picks up and sets down independently. This makes the gait neither diagonal nor lateral, but 'four cornered' or 'square.' Therefore the walk is an even 4-beat gait that sounds like this: 1-2-3-4. All of the intermediate gaits (those gaits that fall between the pace and trot) are actually variations of the walk. For this reason the French used to call the walk "The mother of gaits."

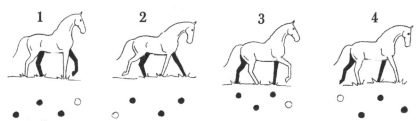

The walk is a square, four-beat gait that forms the basis for all other intermediate (between a pace and a trot) gaits. Here we see the order of footsteps as the horse has just set down it's left hind and prepares to set down the left front (1). As the left front hits the ground, the right hind comes up and moves forward (2). As soon as the right hind sets down, the right front prepares to set down (3). When the right fore leg sets down, the left hind is immediately picked up, to begin the start of the sequence once more.

The Canter

At the canter two diagonal sets of legs move in unison while the other two corner legs move independently of one another. Therefore, the canter is neither a lateral nor a diagonal gait, though two legs do move with diagonal action. As the only three-beat gait, it falls into its own category.

At this gait a horse should move on either the left or right lead, depending upon his direction of travel. This means that when moving on a circle the horse moves the leading, or inside, front and hind legs farther ahead than the non-leading pair in order to keep its balance. This is because a greater proportion of the horse's weight will be leaning toward the center of the circle.

On a right lead canter, the left hind leg is brought under the horse, and he uses it as a kind of springboard as he leaps forward, taking the other three feet off the ground. The right (leading) hind leg reaches deeply under the horse's body and lands on the ground in unison with the left fore leg, which leg balances and steadies the horse as it stretches it's right (leading) foreleg far forward. An instant after the right leading foreleg strikes the ground, the diagonally paired legs come up so that all of the horse's weight is borne on the leading front leg. This is the reason why many people call the inside front leg the leading leg–but actually it is the inside hind leg that provides the most forward impulsion. As the horse's body moves over the inside front leg the left hind sets down once more to help the horse spring forward, and the sequence is repeated.

The canter is a three beat gait with an extra measure of space between each set of footfalls, making it sound uneven, like this: 1-2-3–1-2-3–1-2-3. The order of footfalls at the right lead is: left hind; right hind and left front together; right front. The order is reversed when the horse is traveling on his left lead.

The Gallop

The gallop is always done at speed with the horse stretched full-out, while the canter is a relatively slow collected gait. Otherwise, everything noted above about the order of footfalls at the canter is true of the gallop, with one important exception: at the gallop the two paired diagonal legs land out of synchrony, giving this gait a fast four-beat sound: 1 2 3 4 - 1 2 3 4.

What's so Special about an Intermediate Gait?

What causes some people to prefer gaited saddle horses to the trotting horse is the comfort experienced by the rider. This is because there is no moment of suspension in the horse's gaits. Also the horse's back motion tends to be more forward and back and/or side to side than up and down, thereby reducing concussion between the horse's back and the rider's seat.

Because it is neither too fast, too slow, nor too collected, a non-gaited horse's best ground-covering working gait is usually the trot. But the trot's action creates an up-and-down motion in the back. This, combined with the impact caused by the horse's entire weight landing on the ground after suspension, makes the trot a bouncy, jarring gait. Of course the rider can post the trot by using his ankles, knees and hips as shock absorbers while standing in the stirrups every-other beat. Or he can teach his horse to shuffle along at a less bone-jarring jogging trot, keeping its feet close to the ground. He may learn to soften and relax his back and seat and sit the trot. No matter what, however, it requires patience, physical fitness and skill to ride the trot. No such special qualifications are required to comfortably ride a gaited saddle horse.

If the trot is difficult for a rider to master, the pace is nearly impossible. Besides the up-and-down action and the impact after suspension, the pace has a definite side-to-side swaying motion that can make a rider feel like he's being tossed around on stormy seas. Riding a fast flat pace can make even top notch riders feel like seasick sailors.

Though the flat walk is limiting due to its slow speed, the faster smoother intermediate gaits are little more than variations of the walk, with action sometimes being closer to the trot or pace. During intermediate saddle gaits the rear feet land out of synchrony with the front feet, thus reducing or eliminating suspension. The gaited horse's hind legs may also tend to glide, slide or shuffle forward, rather than land hard and square. These actions reduce concussion between horse and ground, which reduces jarring to the rider.

The Intermediate Gaits

The Amble

If the gait is nearly a pace–same side legs moving in unison–but the hind feet contact the ground an instant before the front feet, then you have a stepping pace, or amble. There is no suspension, fore or hind.

The amble, or stepping pace, is similar to pace, except that hind lateral foot sets down before fore foot. There is no suspension, fore or hind.

Photo: Mickey Anderson

The horse at left is performing an amble, or stepping pace. Note how close the left front foot is to setting down after the left hind has touched the ground.

The Rack

Another specialized gait is the rack which, like the walk and running walk, falls half-way between the two extremes of trot and pace. The primary difference between the two is the length of stride extension. At the running walk, a horse's hind feet oversteps the track of the front feet by at least several inches. At the rack, the hind foot just 'caps' the track of the front foot, or oversteps it just slightly. Also in the rack, the head is carried in a more upright position, with little head nod or shaking. There is usually at least one foot on the ground at all times.

The rack, sometimes called the 'single-foot,' is similar to the running walk, but performed with little or no overstride. There is only moderate head movement as well—while a true running walk always produces a deep head nod.

The Icelandic Horse is known for it's fast rack, called the tolt.

19

Running Walk

If the gait is a walk, but performed so that the hind legs reach, or glide, much deeper under the horse than at the ordinary walk, and at much greater speed, then you have a running walk. Also with the running walk, there is suspension in front, but none behind.

The running walk is similar to a regular walk, but with greater overreach and speed. The hind foot oversteps the track of the fore foot by at least several inches, and the head nods vigorously.

Photo: Mickey Anderson

The running walk. Note the length of hind stride compared to front. It's easy to see why the front legs will need a moment of suspension to keep up! The forefoot comes up just as hind foot sets down.

Fox Trot

If the gait is similar to a trot, but each foreleg lands slightly ahead of the diagonally opposed hind leg, then you have a fox trot. There is suspension behind, but not in front.

The fox trot is a 'broken trot,' ie: the diagonal fore foot sets down an instant before the opposing hind foot.

The fox trot. Here there is obviously no suspension in front, while the hind legs take shorter, higher steps with a moment of suspension between footfalls. This gives the horse the appearance of 'walking in front and trotting behind.'

21

Square Gaits in Motion

Below are some sequential photographs of a Tiger Horse stallion performing his square gait. He moves so easily that the only thing that gives away his speed is the flying mane and tail!

Left hind about to place while left front foot picks up from the ground just ahead of it. Weight borne on right lateral set of legs.

The transition: Left hind has placed. Left front is bent and level with the vertical opposite fore leg, right hind ready to come up. Weight is shifting, and now borne on three legs.

Having completed the transition—Right hind foot firmly down, left fore foot ready to touch the ground. Legs on the opposite side shift into position to repeat the pattern to the other side. Weight is borne on diagonal left front/right hind.

Chapter Two
Types and Conformation

As the last chapter explained, a horse has to both 'wired' and built correctly to be able to perform an intermediate gait. Some horses who have inherited the right nervous system traits for a good intermediate gait perform their gait in a particular manner because of the way they are built.

A rack, for example, has the same footfall characteristics as the running-walk. It's the horse's conformation, or build, that dictates which gait he will more naturally perform.

Most horses that perform a good running-walk are also able to do an acceptable rack and fox-trot. This doesn't always hold true the other way around. Many naturally-gaited racking and fox-trotting horses cannot perform a true running walk because of their physical limitations. They simply don't have the conformation to allow their shoulders to freely roll and their fore and hind structures to obtain great extension of stride. Both qualities are necessary for performing a good running walk.

On the other hand, just because a horse is built in a manner that suggests 'gaitiness' doesn't guarantee that it will gait. It's possible that the animal may not have inherited the necessary nervous system 'wiring' to gait. So you need to consider the horse's genetic heritage, as well as its conformation. Usually if an animal

The best way to be absolutely certain an unproven horse will consistently gait is to make sure it is descended from gaited parents. Naturally gaited foals demonstrate intermediate gaits at their dam's side.

Photo courtesy of Pascale Smith

comes from a gaited sire and/or dam, and exhibits the right kind of conformation, that horse will gait, given the right training. Nevertheless, the only way to be certain a horse possesses the ability for an intermediate gait is to watch it actually perform.

The Spanish Type Horse

Gaited horses come in many types and sizes which can be divided into two primary types: Spanish, and English. Horses of primarily Spanish origin (pasos, and 'Colonial' horses) often tend toward the lateral gaits, such as the stepping pace, or amble. They generally stand 15 hands high or less. They possess tightly coupled loins and smooth, well-rounded muscles. This is particularly evident in the croup, which is usually very round—sometimes even apple shaped. Don't let the round muscling fool you! Regardless of how well-rounded the croup, the underlying bone structure of the pelvis should be sloping.

Spanish type horses may have heavy necks, set into a deep to medium-sloped shoulder. They generally have a naturally high head carriage and carry their proud, finely-chiseled, expressive heads with the nose pointed slightly up and out, even when gaiting under saddle.

The front legs of these horses are sturdy, but refined, and spring directly from a broad, well-muscled chest and shoulder. They are deep and round through the body, with an underline slightly longer than the top-line. As with other truly well-balanced horses, the ideal horse will be nearly equally divided three ways: head to wither/back to loin/loin to tail. In addition, the heart-girth may be as deep as the back is long (rear-wither to loin), and the front legs as long as the body is deep (through the cinch area).

The hind legs of a gaited Spanish-type horse are lengthy and well angled—so much so that often they appear to be slightly cow-hocked. Both front and rear pasterns are medium to long in length, and exhibit average to deep angulation.

This type of horse usually carries itself in a smooth, quick manner. Even when collected, it's head will be forward of the vertical, and its back may appear slightly hollow. When in motion, most of the action appears to be in the legs, so that there is only slight to moderate head nod and shoulder and hip motion.

A typical Spanish type horse.

Our friendly model, Showme, demonstrates the ideal proportions of a well-balanced horse. Dividing him into thirds lengthwise gives him one-third of his length from chest to wither, one-third from wither to loin, and one-third from loin to point of buttock.

The one-third rule of conformation is again demonstrated. The ideal horse's back, heart-girth and length of front leg should be approximately equal.

The horse's topline should be shorter than it's bottom line. Too short on the bottom, and a gaited horse will be very inclined to forge, or hit his front feet with his back feet.

Even if the horse's legs should be clean and straight—which they should be—on occasion you might find an animal that exhibits 'termino.' This is a Spanish characteristic whereby the horse's foot appears to 'wing' or 'paddle' with each stride. If it is true termino, the motion will originate in the shoulder and the feet will land squarely on the ground. Both front legs will exhibit the action, and not just one. Termino is not a result of, nor does it indicate, any conformational fault. It is considered a desirable characteristic among Peruvian Pasos.

If you're looking for a trail and pleasure horse that will give you a smooth, ground-covering stride, then you'll want to be careful not to buy a Paso Fino horse that has been specifically bred to perform the show ring Paso Fino (or fine step) gait. This kind of horse is bred for, and judged upon, its ability to move forward with very small, rapid steps, exhibiting little forward extension. A

horse with the conformation to perform the gait well will not likely also possess a well-extended ground covering gait, for the two gaits call for entirely different conformation standards.

Spanish style gaited horses are often very sure-footed and handy, and can traverse rocky and mountainous terrain with apparent ease. They excel at traveling over rough trails and uncharted territory, and often seem to love the challenge of this type of riding. A good Spanish-type horse, on the whole, is spirited, sturdy, trustworthy and efficient. He

This Peruvian Paso is demonstrating true termino. Note how the right front leg rolls out sideways from the shoulder.

27

The Paso Fino show gait is very quick and smooth, but the horse that has been bred to perform the 'fino', or fine-stepping show gait, may not be the best choice for a durable trail horse. However, Spanish gaited stock with a good 'paso largo' gait—equivalent to the rack or running walk—are often excellent trail and utility mounts.

can commonly carry greater weight in proportion to his size than can other kinds of horses.

This kind of animal is especially suited to riding where the terrain, as opposed to distance, is the primary challenge. While they have been known to travel long distances, their smaller size and the way they work their fine legs (hard!) may contribute to early breakdown if they are frequently ridden at speed over long distances.

Of course, there are so many variables within any given type that what may be true for one type of gaited horse as a whole may not be at all true for a particular individual or sub-type within that spectrum. Peruvian Pasos, for example, are gaited Spanish horses that have been known to travel clear across the Americas!

The English Type Horse

English type gaited horses are usually taller than their Spanish counterparts, standing between 15 and 16.2 hands high. As a rule they are bred to perform the true intermediate gaits (running-walk and rack), as well as the more diagonal fox-trot. Unfortunately, artificial show-ring standards and less-than-ethical breeding practices have caused many of these horses to inherit a strong tendency to pace. This is a problem diligently being addressed by

An English type horse.

a number of breeders who appreciate the unique characteristics of the genuine racking, run-walking and fox-trotting horses.

English type horses are not only taller, but tend to be rangier than their Spanish counterparts. The shoulders and loins boast deeply sloping angles, long legs exhibit good bone with large, well-defined joints. Sturdy pasterns are short to medium in length, and rest atop a large, well-balanced foot. The head has an elongated straight profile. The neck is medium to long and often set into the shoulder quite high—not uncommonly right into a well-defined wither.

As with any type of horse, a short back is the ideal. But in practical use a long back can be compensated for if the coupling between the back and hind end is tight, short and strong. In such a case the horse shouldn't experience undue physical stress even if it has a fairly long back. Some long-backed horses have a comfortably soft, rolling action under saddle that is a delight to ride. They are, however, often inclined to pace.

If a horse possesses a long back combined with long, weak coupling, it will always be a challenge to train that horse to coil at the loins to move in the correct frame. This problem is exacerbated when the hind legs are either too straight or too long. Too

29

Showme's back has become too long. This, especially when combined with weak coupling at the loins, is likely to lead to early breakdown. (Horses built this way frequently have a strong tendency to perform a flat pace.)

much straightness will make the horse choppy and uncomfortable to ride, and contribute to early breakdown. Too much hind-leg length, combined with the weak loin, will make it even more difficult for the horse to collect in a nice, round frame. Some horses with this fault are never able to generate enough collected impulsion to lope or canter. They also can carry less weight in proportion to their size.

When considering a horse of the English body type, you'll usually find that their entire bodies contribute to the gaits they perform. A Walking Horse moving in good form will have an extremely loose movement. He will reach so deeply underneath with his hind legs that his hip and thigh muscles will actually stretch with the effort. His shoulder rolls smoothly and loosely with his front leg action and his head nods deeply with each stride. Only the rider, seated midpoint on his back, is kept in a non-moving state!

A good loose-moving Walking Horse often reminds me of a gate, opening and closing, as he strolls across the ground. Some old-timers call this action 'pushing and pulling,' as the horse pushes himself vigorously forward with his hind legs and pulls himself forward with his front legs.

The Fox Trotter, while not usually as loose as the Walking Horse behind, nevertheless will have a quick head nod and piston-like action in the hind end, and his shoulder will stretch as he reaches far forward with his front foot. Sometimes the head moves so vigorously that you can hear a distinct 'clack-clack' noise as the horse's upper and lower teeth bounce on one another with each stride!

The Racking Horse also exhibits body motion under saddle, with a moderately nodding head and swinging back end. For the purposes of this book, we are considering only the lower-stepping, more relaxed rack, as opposed to the Saddlebred show rack.

English type horses, overall, excel at long-distance riding. They can really 'hit a lick' when asked to cover smooth roads and trails at speed, and seem to be able to go on forever! Though reasonably sure-footed, they aren't always as handy over extremely rough terrain as their Spanish counterparts. They compensate for this by being very competent hunter/jumpers and cross-country mounts.

Some show-lines of Missouri Fox Trotters and Tennessee Walking Horses do not exhibit the sure-footedness to be desired and expected in naturally gaited horses. This is because some MFT breeders have been overemphasizing the low-slung reach in the front legs to a point that's become ludicrous. A horse that is bred so that its conformation prevents it from picking up its legs more than an inch or two in front is going to be in trouble when asked to travel over rough ground. Likewise many TWH show horses have been bred to move their hind legs in an exaggeratedly low way beneath them, making them more likely to stumble in the rear. They also are primarily bred for a strong pace, so that it will perform the absurd and totally unnatural 'Big Lick' show gait when sored and/or fitted with pads, weights and heavy shoes. Besides

31

Photo by Mickey Anderson

A good running walk demonstrates a reaching stride behind with a pulling action in front.

the problem of stumbling, horses that pace tend to be very uncomfortable and unsafe when traveling down hills, and may tend to cross-canter (if they canter at all), another unsafe situation.

Purchasing a show-quality Racking Horse is also no guarantee of acquiring an appropriate trail mount. Show ring trends that favor exaggerated action and high-headed 'spirit' produce animals of uncertain temperament that quickly tire on the trail. Over time they may simply wear out quicker than their more humbly bred cousins.

I can already hear the cries of 'foul!' as fans of these kinds of horses race to inform me that their horses can do anything any other horse can do—and better! To a large extent this is true. It's even more true in the case of particular horses. But it's my intent to give an honest overview to those who don't have any idea about what to expect, or what to look for, when they go shopping for a gaited horse. I think the above explanations and limitations are faithful to that end.

Crossover Types

We've covered the two primary general types of gaited horses, Spanish and English. There is, however, another kind of horse that is a hybrid of the two. These horses often hail from the Ozarks and other southern mountainous regions of the United States, and are a result of crossing early Spanish gaited stock with the American Saddlebred. Commonly these are known as 'mountain horses' of one kind or another–though there's a large percentage of such horses included among Missouri Fox Trotters, as well as some registered Tennessee Walking Horses. It's not uncommon to see the straight profile and long neck of the English type horse setting on an animal with a very rounded, compact Spanish type body. Conversely, I've seen the finely chiseled head and heavy neck of the Spanish type horse coupled with a long, lean English type body. Almost any combination is possible with these kinds of horses!

Given the recent flush of popularity of the gaited 'mountain horse,' it is especially prudent when considering the purchase of such a horse to be absolutely certain that it can perform an intermediate gait. Don't be overly swayed by color standards when hunting for a horse in this market. To meet market trends and demands for exotic color there has been a great deal of outcrossing to non-gaited stock over the past several years, resulting in a sometimes unreliable gene pool. You needn't be afraid to enter this market, as it can be rewarding both personally and financially. But go in with your eyes wide open, and ask *lots* of questions before you lay out your hard-earned cash!

One woman called me several months ago asking for advice and seeking reassurance about her beautiful, chocolate-colored mountain bred 2-year-old gelding. She'd purchased the horse as a weanling, impressed by the breeder's claims as to its smooth gaits and sure-footedness. The next year she purchased his full sister as an investment. When she called me, she had yet to witness either horse perform anything other than a trot. Indeed, she'd started riding her gelding, and nothing her trainer did could induce him to take up an intermediate gait. She wanted to know if there was some special trick she could use to get her horse to perform the

Merry Boy's Spirit F-88 demonstrates characteristics common to both Spanish and English type gaited horses.

natural gait she'd been told was inherited 100% of the time among this particular breed of horse.

After talking to her for several minutes it seemed evident that she had purchased an unproven horse of unproven lines that would probably never live up to her expectations. Imagine my consternation when she consoled herself out loud with the prospect of recouping her investment by breeding her equally unproven–but popularly colored–mare for this burgeoning market!

Am I saying the mountain type gaited horses aren't good prospects? Not at all. There are some excellent breeders and horses in this market. I'm hoping to impress upon you the necessity to do your homework, and check any horse out carefully before you buy, regardless of breed or type. There are a great many horses on the market with an unreliable–even unethical–gaited heritage. Who but the unwary, inexperienced buyer of gaited stock is likely to purchase such an animal? That buyer is bound to be disappointed, and perhaps to turn sour on gaited horses altogether. This reflects poorly on the entire industry, and limits the marketability of our very special type of horses.

General Conformation Standards

Shoulder and Arm

There's a great deal of variance on the conformation of a gaited horse's shoulder. Some horses have deeply sloping shoulders or scapula, while others are relatively upright. Either type of conformation can allow for acceptable gait–so long as the horse is well balanced, back to front, and the humerus (arm bone) is of acceptable length and angle. As a rule, the more deeply angled the shoulder, the more reach the horse will have in front. The longer the length, and the more upright the angle of the humerus, the higher the horse will be able to lift its front feet.

While reach is important, so is lift. To determine if the horse will have both acceptable front stride length and the ability to lift his legs, we need to observe how the shoulder is sloped in relation to the humerus, as well as how steep and long the arm is in comparison to the shoulder.

Ideally the arm (humerus) will be at least 50% of the length of the shoulder–75% isn't too long. The shorter the arm, the shorter and choppier the gait is likely to be. The longer the arm–and the more vertically positioned, the more 'scope' or rolling reach, the horse will have.

Scapula

Humerus

This drawing illustrates the relationship of the scapula (shoulder bone) to the humerus (arm bone). The length and angulation of these largely determines how the horse will move and balance itself in front.

35

Above and below: Mickey Anderson

Though each one of these horses exhibits different body types, the underlying shoulder structure in each is fine for gaited motion. Notice the lengths and angles in relation to one another. It's a good idea to look at many horses with an eye to the underlying structure, until you can tell without even thinking about it whether or not a horse is likely to demonstrate good scope and motion in the front end.

If you draw an imaginary line from the shoulder down through the point of wither to the ground, you'll get a good idea of the horse's potential length of stride. Now imagine the arm bone 'closing' up to the underside of the scapula as he lifts his leg. This will give you an idea about how much elevation the horse can achieve. Note where the scapula joins the arm (point of shoulder). The lower this point, the lower the horse will carry his head. The higher this point, the higher the horse will carry his head.

Conformation structure can be seen even in very young horses. The skeletal angles tend to remain fairly constant, though the horse may appear 'gangly' or grow unevenly from back to front from time to time. Note the beautiful angles on this ten-month-old Tennessee Walker.

In the best of all worlds there will be approximately a 90° angle between the arm and shoulder. This means that if the shoulder has a 45° slope, then the arm should have a 45° angle as well. If the horse's shoulder slopes to 50°, then the humerus needs to be slightly more upright at about 40°. As you can see, there's a great deal of tolerable deviation. But there are also reasonable limitations to these 'rules.'

For one thing, if the humerus has a very horizontal angle–say 30° or less–then the horse will tend to carry its head low and have limited lift in front. He'll be front-heavy, hard to collect–and probably not very smooth–gaited as a result. This is even more true if the slope of the shoulder isn't at least 60° to compensate for the poor arm angle.

While it would be difficult to get a shoulder that is too sloping, it isn't uncommon to find one too steep. This seriously hinders the length of stride. A straight line drawn from the point of the horse's withers, through the point of shoulder and down to the ground will demonstrate how far the horse can extend. A horse with poor extension may be able to gait, but will have to take many short strides to cover the same ground as a horse with a more sloping shoulder. This makes the gait choppier and is extremely hard on the horse–which may lead to early breakdown.

Gaits of Gold

If you draw an imaginary line from the horse's withers, down through the point of shoulder to the ground, you'll get a good idea about the horse's natural length of stride. Here we draw the line with the horse in motion, to demonstrate that the angle of the shoulder accurately predicts the length of stride. If you see the horse reaching far beyond this point, as in the bottom photo, you may be fairly certain that artificial training and/or shoeing devices have been employed to change the animal's natural way of going.

Photos: Mickey Anderson

38

Rear End Conformation

An important conformational signpost of a gaited horse, regardless of general type or origin, is its back end. Look for a horse with strong coupling between the back, groin and hip, and a moderately long, deeply sloped pelvis. There is often a more open angle formed between the pelvis and stifle joints (pelvis and femur bone) than what is seen in non-gaited horses. As with the shoulder and arm, an angle of approximately 90° is excellent. Any less than this, and the angle is too closed to allow the joints to 'swing shut' enough to give the horse a strong under-reach. If it's much more open than this the horse will tend to travel with his hocks 'strung out' behind him, and lack good propulsion. It may also contribute to hind-end stumbling.

In addition, a good Walking Horse in particular will tend to have a relatively long femur bone. The gaskins of all types of gaited horses should be as long, or slightly longer than, the femur.

This ideal angle between the pelvis and femur bone, combined with a long gaskin, enables the animal to freely swing it's

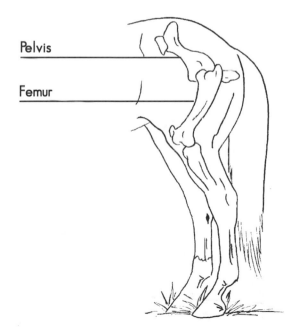

Pelvis

Femur

The femur of a gaited horse should be long in relation to its pelvis. In addition, it should have a gaskin as long as—or longer than—the femur bone.

long hind legs deeply beneath its body. Along with this conformational hallmark, there's a certain loose-jointedness that the gaited horse buyer soon learns to look for and recognize as well.

A horse with a long femur will have a proportionally long hamstring, which should tie in below the stifle joint. The hallmark of this desirable gaited horse trait is the appearance (from a side profile view) of a long, flowing, taut appearance from the point of hip to the bottom of the gaskin. While this may sound complicated to understand, the photo of the MFT Froghorn's Quivera (below) will clearly demonstrate what I'm trying to describe. Horses with this conformation trait will almost surely gait—though there's no guarantee that the gait won't be a strong pace! Some types of gaited

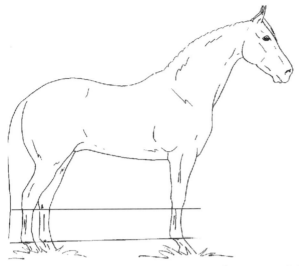

Showme's hind cannons are nearly equal in length to his fore cannons. This causes his hocks to be set low, which helps him to achieve good stride length and balance.

horses have enough muscle over this area of the loin to disguise the underlying structures—but you should be able to detect them, with practice.

As mentioned, ideally a gaited horse's hind legs are slightly longer than usual, largely due to the long gaskin. If it is the cannon bone which is long, paired with an average or short femur and gaskin, then you'll be looking at a short-strided horse that will travel in an unbalanced 'downhill' fashion. The hind cannon bone should be only slightly longer than the front, giving the horse low-set hocks. This will contribute to the animal's ability set his hocks well underneath himself.

With this kind of conformation the horse will stand level with its legs well underneath itself, rather than tending to stand 'butt up and downhill,' placing too much weight on its front legs. Of course, the horse may have been trained to stand parked out with its hind legs stretched behind itself when being examined/handled. A young horse may stand downhill following a growth spurt. But a mature horse that habitually travels downhill will be difficult to ride and work with.

When I say that the horse should have a sloping pelvis, I am talking about the underlying bone structure, and not the muscula-ture 'dressing' over that structure. Train your eye to see the horse's

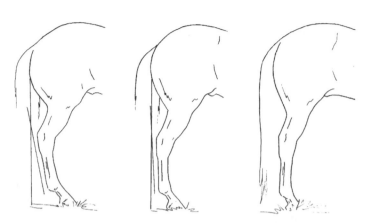

Gaited stock generally have longer hind limbs than non-gaited, but this should not be taken to extremes. The drawing on the left demonstrates a horse with too-long hind cannons, resulting in sickle hocks. The center illustration shows acceptable length and angle for a gaited horse, while the inside drawing shows a 'post-legged' horse, i.e.: one with too little length and angle in its hind limbs.

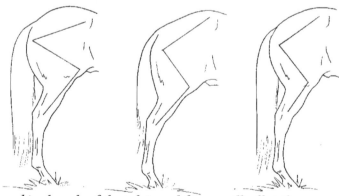

The combined angle of the pelvis and femur will affect the way a horse moves. If the angle is too closed, as in the illustration on the left, the horse will have shorter, choppier gaits. A too-open angle (center) will make it difficult for the horse to collect. Such a horse will tend to move in a strung out manner, it's legs trailing behind, which makes cantering difficult. The outside illustration shows the ideal length and angle.

At right are three breeds of
gaited horses: Tennessee
Walking Horse, Missouri
Fox Trotter, and Paso Fino
(top to bottom). Each has
beautiful conformation.
Though of different breeding
and overall body types, the
basic conformational
standards that make for
strength, soundness and
good gaited action are
demonstrated in each horse.

Mickey Anderson

Note the shoulder and loin
angles on each horse, and
how well balanced they are,
front to back. The topline is
shorter than the bottom line
in each horse, and their
proportions follow the 1/3
rules. They exhibit good
bone, being neither too
heavy nor too refined in the
legs, and they each have
hocks set on fairly low.

Study these photos in light
of the lessons in this
chapter, to see if you can
picture in your mind how
each horse would be likely
to move under saddle.

underlying structure. Some English type horses have been bred to have a flat croup—yet their pelvis exhibits the necessary angle to create gait ability. The same holds true for the rounded croup, deeply angled pelvis of Spanish type horses.

Then there are the horses whose croups drop off suddenly, following the true angle of the pelvis. These horses may be faulted for being too light in the back end—yet they usually prove to be just as strong and durable as their more muscular relatives. This is because the 'power-drive' of a horse originates in the back and loins, and not from the croup. Those who are accustomed to seeing the heavily-muscled American Quarterhorse might be put off by the light muscling and angulation of the hind end of a Tennessee Walking Horse (for example). Don't be too hard on such a horse until you've had a chance to enjoy its ride! You'll probably find a whole new appreciation for this kind of conformation once you've experienced its benefits.

If your goal is to own a horse or horses with durability, sure-footedness, and comfort for trail and pleasure riding, then it is wise to overlook certain market and show ring trends and stick to buying horses that demonstrate good old-fashioned conformational qualities—even if they're not considered 'pretty' by show ring or market trend standards. Over the long term you'll learn the wisdom of the saying: 'Pretty is as pretty does.'

Besides this, what is considered attractive is culturally determined. In the United States we are largely accustomed to seeing the Quarter Horse depicted as the ideal type, and so any variance from that seems odd or unattractive. But as gaited horses continue to gain in popularity, we will begin to see them in a more favorable light.

In particular I want to address the misconception that Walking Horses have big, ugly heads. While it's true that some of the horses in this breed lack true refinement—which is true of *all* breeds—it's also true that wonderfully refined Walking Horses often have larger heads and straighter profiles than some other kinds of horses. This doesn't make them common, or unattractive. It merely gives them an expressive, noble—and often very individualistic—look that is extremely becoming, once you grow accustomed to it. I'd hate to see TWH breeders making small, modeled Arab-type heads one of their primary breeding goals–though I fear that's already happening to some degree. Instead of changing breed standards to suit the current fashion, let's learn to appreciate our horses for what they are. . .each uniquely interesting and beautiful.

Chapter Three
Still Looking. . .

So now you have some sense of what to look for in the conformation of a gaited horse—but there are many other factors to consider as well. Many of these are things that apply to any kind of riding horse, others more specifically to gaited horses.

Good Horse Sources

When considering the purchase of a gaited horse, be certain you are dealing with a breeder who has a strong reputation for producing naturally-gaited pleasure horses. He or she should be *passionate* on this subject! If you plan to use the horse for trail and pleasure, then be somewhat wary of big show barns and modern show breeding lines. The exception to this would be barns/trainers who are obviously proud of producing top-quality lite-shod horses.

You might also be very careful if planning to purchase a horse at auction. Many gaited horse 'culls' show up at auction, to be purchased by folks who don't understand what makes for a great gaited horse. They simply hope to get a good horse at a cheap price. All too often, what they've actually paid for is an education—

they quickly learn that there are few things more miserable than a horse that won't or can't do what it's supposed to do. Of course there are reputable auctions as well. Just be well aware of the differences—unless of course you're one of those rare individuals who possess a foolproof eye for a good horse.

Soundness

Of prime consideration when purchasing a horse is the question: will it go sound? Essentially this means that the horse's legs, feet and breathing apparatus are all in good workable order.

Initially you only have to determine that the horse isn't limping at any gait, there are no scars and/or lumps at its joints, and its breathing isn't obviously labored. Later, if you decide you are definitely interested in purchasing the animal, by all means insist on a vet check **using a vet of your choice**, and not the seller's. Most reputable auction barns will have an objective vet on the premises.

Price

Too often folks decide to purchase a horse, and set an unreasonable limitation on what they will pay for the animal. This is especially true for those who plan to purchase 'only' a trail horse. They think that just because the horse isn't going to be strutting it's fancy self in the show ring, it won't have a very high value. Untrue, and unfair—to both horses and breeders/trainers.

A good trail horse—especially a good, sound *gaited* trail horse—can be hard to find. Such an animal needs to be well-trained to saddle and to gait, to be responsive, levelheaded and sure-footed, have stamina and courage, and get along well under all kinds of circumstances and with all kinds of horses. It can't be prone to stumble, spook or panic. He needs to be willing to cross uncertain terrain, though all his instincts cue him otherwise. A trail horse needs a strong, durable conformation, and should be well-conditioned. If another horse suddenly comes up behind him, the good trail horse takes it in stride. It requires good breeding and training—plus many, many hours and miles of riding—to produce this

Cody's Mustard Man takes owner Rex Walker calmly through water. Looks, and is, simple—once the horse has the right basic training. If you don't want to put that much time in to produce a trail horse, you should plan to pay a fair price to someone who has.

kind of horse. There are no overnight wonders, nor training short-cuts that can be taken.

All too often, purchasers set the arbitrary price limit of $1500.00, and refuse to consider any horse that sells for more. What a mistake this can be! Often such purchasers end up paying more for their 'cheap' horse over the long run than if they'd spent more on a more appropriate, seasoned mount in the first place. They may need to pay for extra training—or for doctor bills when the horse dumps them in a frightening situation. The horse may be unconditioned, and/or go unsound—and this will almost always happen in the worst possible place.

I recall a ride that included a man whose inexpensive older trail horse went lame halfway into a long backwoods ride. He probably had plenty of time to wonder if he'd gotten such a great deal on the animal as he walked the horse more than five miles home, through mountainous terrain!

Gaits of Gold

A few considerations when determining the financial value of the horse. At left, this kind gelding helped his little mistress make some lifetime memories. What is this kind of gentle kindness worth to a parent who is horse shopping for their child?

At right and below. Trail horses need many special qualities. If the horse is spirited, can you handle its early-morning trail excitement with ease? Does the horse calmly accept other animals coming up too close behind?

Photos by Mickey Anderson

I made this mistake when purchasing a horse one time. He ended up suffering from heaves. He was usually just fine, but often would come up sick the very day of a ride. He also had several bad habits that we learned to contend with–usually the hard way. We ended up loving and keeping this game old fellow. But we didn't make peace with him overnight–and it cost us plenty over the long run. Another thousand dollars invested at the outset for a less complicated horse would have been money well spent.

So please don't make the mistake of limiting yourself only to 'cheap' animals. Consider all that goes into the making of a good gaited horse, and be willing to pay a fair and reasonable price.

What is reasonable? That depends. Are you willing to do some, or most, of the hard conditioning, training and riding work yourself–or is your time and/or experience limited? Do you want a mare that will produce a nice offspring for you sometime in the future? Are you set on getting a fancy coat color–spotted or palomino, for example?

All of these things will have a bearing on the purchase price of the horse. If you have the time and ability to purchase a very young horse and bring it along yourself, then perhaps $1500.00 isn't an unreasonable goal. On the other hand, if you want to purchase a breeding quality mare, that's going to add to the value– perhaps another thousand or fifteen hundred dollars, depending on her age, condition and training. Spotted Saddle Horses (gaited pintos) are in great demand–as are some of the fancier colored 'mountain horses' and *all* kinds of champagne and palomino horses. Expect to pay in excess of $3,000.00 for one of these, fairly well trained. More if it's potential breeding stock. Still more if it's well-gaited, well-trained, and in its prime (between 5 and 8 years of age).

Sound too rich for your blood? Consider this: a good, well-kept horse should give you at least 15 years of pleasure. If you initially pay (for example) $3000.00 for such a horse, then that works out to $200.00 per year. On the other hand, your second automobile–or RV or SUV–probably cost in excess of $15000.00. You'll be lucky if it serves you a half-dozen years. I use the word 'serve' loosely–only a living, breathing horse will really *serve* you,

Photo by Mickey Anderson

While you won't actually be marrying your horse purchase, you'll probably need to learn to get along for a very long time. Starting out with the right 'mate' will make the adjustment much easier!

with its heart! That's a cost of $2500.00 per year–*or over ten times as much money.* Both need to be housed, maintained, kept in fuel, etc. Now I ask, which is the better deal?

Temperament

Temperament is a prime factor when considering a horse for purchase. Few things are more distracting and miserable than getting an animal that blows up at the slightest provocation, is continually unwilling and sour, or who simply can't get along with other horses. No matter how smooth a horse may be to ride, life with a 1,000+ pound beast that has serious temperamental flaws will be anything **but** smooth!

Of course, some types of character traits aren't immediately evident in the space of time we have for evaluating a prospect. This is especially true when purchasing a horse at auction. We can stack the odds in our favor if we know what to look for, and how to assess the animal as well as possible under restrictive conditions.

I always watch the horse with his current handler, of course– but it helps to watch the handler just as closely. Does she seem nervous or afraid around the horse? Ask to see the horse's mouth, ears and feet being handled. Does the handler seem especially cautious around the mouth or back legs? Does the horse fight any of these routine procedures? (Some horses may object to having their mouths handled. This, however, should be a relatively mild objection, and not a violent rearing or head-butting affair.)

Is there a constant chatter going on while the handler makes subtle nervous apologies for 'minor problems' the horse might exhibit? Or does he/she speak with apparent ease and authority to, and about, the animal?

Is the handler willing to tack up and ride the horse without hesitation? Once on the horse, does she seem confident and unafraid? Will she ride the horse in an open place–or only in a restricted arena or round pen? Will she take the horse through all the gaits–even the lope or canter?

Does the current owner seem to have a good grasp of the animal's background regarding breeding, training and experience, without probable exaggeration, given the horse and its price range?

When the horse is led out past other animals, does it demonstrate obviously aggressive behavior (snaking its head, pinning its ears, attempting to bite or kick)? If so, beware. You need a horse that will be accepting of other horses. Does it run past the other horses in evident fear, jumping out of range for no apparent reason? Does it call out and fight being ridden and/or led away from the barn and its herd mates? Herd bound horses are difficult to deal with–and can be downright dangerous. Most can be retrained, but there are a few who never get over this inclination.

If the horse is to be turned out with others while in your possession (a good idea for any horse!) ask to see it turned out with its current pasture-mates, if possible. Also look him over to see if he has a number of kick/bite marks on his body, indicating he's 'low man' in the herd pecking order. Such a horse will require special consideration all its life. A horse that is either too aggressive or too timid with other horses can be a major headache to own.

Watch the horse in the stall, and in the pasture. Does he stand quietly, eating grass or hay? Or does he stand in a corner, head down, looking dispirited and depressed? Is he easy to catch and handle from the pasture? In his stall, does he pace nervously, or weave, or indulge in cribbing or wind-sucking? (Both of these are a nervous disorder whereby the horse either grabs hold of the edge of a surface–or its own tongue–with its teeth, sucks in air, and makes a disgusting 'burp' sound.) Check the stall itself: does it look like it's been badly kicked, chewed or otherwise used by a horse with problems?

Serious wood chewers can literally eat their way through the average wood stall in a few days' time, keeping their owners busier with hammer and nails than with saddle and bridle. Habitual stall kickers not only wreak havoc on their stalls, but on their hind legs as well. Stall kickers often exhibit swollen hocks. Horses that pace and weave will definitely be expensive to feed, and will simply wear out sooner than usual. Cribbers and wind-suckers can be perfectly fine horses, but may be unthrifty to keep. Cribbers tend to wear their front teeth down faster than average, causing them to under-utilize their food.

Many horse breeders avoid acquiring horses with these vices because they believe the behaviors are inherited, 'contagious' to the rest of the herd, or both. It does seem true at least that foals are born with a strong predisposition to demonstrate their dam's vices. In any event, over time these kinds of vices in a horse may drive you up a wall!

On a personal note, however, a very nice gelding I once owned was an inveterate wind-sucker. He never practiced the vice while under saddle, and was so well-suited for me in other regards that it was easy to overlook this shortcoming. Though many other horses were kept in close proximity with him, none of them ever acquired the habit.

Which is my not-so-subtle way of saying that, while we **look** for perfection, few such creatures exist in the real world. If a horse meets our needs in many other respects, we shouldn't automatically rule it out because of a relatively harmless vice. As with most worthwhile ventures in life, we need to carefully weigh the good against the bad.

A horse that likes, trusts and respects people is a delight to have around–make every effort to determine if this is the case with the one you're evaluating. Does the animal have a bright, inquisitive expression, and a soft eye? Does its body language toward you and the handler suggest that it will respect your personal space? Is it mannerly when being led? When someone comes into its stall? While eating? Some horses get downright vicious during feeding time, and you'll need to understand and accommodate this behavior, as it usually cannot be altered.

Ask to see the horse loaded onto a trailer if possible. Does it load easily, and stand quietly inside? Will it unload in a cautious, safe manner—as opposed to rearing off the trailer, or shooting off backward like a speeding bullet? Few things are more frustrating than having a horse that fights loading, traveling and unloading. If

you purchase such an animal, plan to spend some time retraining it, or paying to have it retrained professionally. Make sure that the horse will not only load in a nice roomy stock trailer, but in a vehicle similar to one you'll actually be using.

My own recent experience might serve as a warning. I purchased a lovely Tennessee Walking Horse

Carefully observe the horse. Does it demonstrate a kind and gentle nature—or does it appear difficult and temperamental?

gelding, 16.1 hands high and weighing over 1200 pounds. (I was looking for a small broodmare. . .but that's another story!)

While this horse wasn't perfect, he possessed so many good qualities that I decided to purchase him and send him to a qualified trainer to work out a few obvious 'kinks'. It was apparent that this big guy really *liked* people, which weighed heavily into my decision to purchase. He also seemed to have a level head and good basic training under saddle. But the clincher on this deal was that he possessed *outstanding* saddle gaits.

He was, however, seriously barn-sour. Normally this would have dampened any enthusiasm I had for him, but I'd brought a knowledgeable trainer with me (always a good idea). She was able to ride the horse away from the barn within a relatively short time–and she really wanted me to purchase this horse! Since she's familiar with my capabilities, and I trust her judgement–and the price was right–I agreed to give this big guy a try.

He loaded, traveled and unloaded from her stock trailer just fine. In fact, he was even good when I used a step-up two-horse trailer to bring him home from the trainer's. Over just a few weeks' time, with my trainer's help, we had worked out all his problems. Or so it seemed.

But early this year I bought a two-horse, ramp-load trailer. Never gave it a thought–until the day of my first big trail-ride. Everything seemed set to go. We'd been riding and conditioning in the hills surrounding our house. He got along fine with friends' horses, and was getting downright handy on the trail. The day of the big ride I got up extra early in the morning, gave him a good grooming, loaded all my gear into the truck, hitched it to the trailer, and led him out to load up. Ever try to wrestle a 1200+ pound horse into a standing-stall sized space against its will?

I never did make the ride that day. By the time two inexperienced helpers and I finally got him onto the trailer, it was too late to go–and I had a nasty brush burn across my face. (I won't bore you with the sad details.) That was early in the riding season. It took several weeks to get him completely over this problem. During that time, I arrived at every ride already exhausted. Then

I had to enlist the aid of kind men to help me get him back on the trailer to take home. Now, he loads like a dream—but it didn't come easy!

Would I have purchased him if I'd known about this strong aversion? Hard to tell. But it would have been nice to know about it ahead of time. At the least, I could have worked it out beforehand, maybe with my trainer's help, rather than being caught alone and unprepared at an inopportune time.

These are the kinds of things that can throw a snafu into the best-seeming horse deals. So don't be hurried into a purchase decision. As much as possible take your time and make certain that the horse will actually do all the things required of him once you get him home. If you shortchange yourself during the evaluation process, you could be paying for it over a very long time, in more ways than one. When purchasing horses the old proverb is doubly true: "Act in haste, repent at leisure."

If the horse has pleased you so far, and you're buying it at least partly for use on the trail, then if possible go out on the trail with it. At the very least, check to make sure that waving plastic, opening umbrellas and the like don't sent it to the moon. Some lines of Tennessee Walking Horses, in particular, tend to be quite sensitive and spooky until they're older and well-experienced (in my humble opinion). Ask permission from the owner/rider before bringing out any of these bugaboos, so you don't inadvertently cause a sudden reaction that will send the rider flying. The opened umbrella is especially useful if you plan to do any showing, since eventually some ringside spectator will surely open one, "whoosh!" right under your horse's nose on a wet and slippery show day.

Expect the horse to show some reaction to these things. What you're looking for is *how violently and persistently* he will respond to such stimuli. Is his attitude one of mild interest, perhaps taking a step or two sideways? Does his response become calmer each time he's exposed to the bugaboo—or does he persistently blow up each time he's faced with the provocation? Perhaps even becoming worse? A horse that persistently blows out of its rider's control when confronted with a moderately frightening situation is unlikely to change. As a rule, this is a temperamental problem that will cause a great amount of grief over time. Some horses may be professionally retrained to modify their reactions–modify being the key word. They'll probably always be highly reactionary animals, regardless of experience or training. Just so you know.

Know Thyself. . .

Which brings us to our next point: make certain that the horse is temperamentally suited to your personality, and to your riding skill level. As a rule, gaited horses *do* move and respond to things a bit faster than their non-gaited counterparts. I believe they tend to be more spirited, overall. But they are also easier to *stay with* than non-gaited horses. I've ridden gaited horses who moved like greased lightening, and been much less challenged than I have been by certain jarring, hard-going trotting horses. So try to overlook speed, and concentrate on the horse's *reactivity* and manner of responding to stimuli.

Are you an experienced, athletic and agile rider who's not intimidated by an occasional hard spook and who enjoys the excitement and challenge of riding a highly spirited horse? Don't settle for an animal that has wonderfully long, smooth strides–but who is a real quiet 'steady Freddy' temperamentally. Chances are good that you'll be bored with such a horse in no time flat.

If you're a bit uncertain about your ability to handle a spirited horse–experience notwithstanding–and the prospect makes you more uptight than excited, then don't settle for a horse until you've found one that will be quiet and dependable. This probably means you'll want a well-trained older horse–mid-teens isn't too old, if the horse is sound. You may eventually get bored. Better to be bored than injured, or turned off of horses altogether. You can always move up to a more spirited horse when you've gained experience and confidence. If you want.

One thing I wish I could impress on horse lovers' brains–*we don't have to prove anything to anybody!* I find there's often entirely too much 'one-upmanship' among horse people of all disciplines.

Nothing substitutes for having good 'chemistry' with the horse you purchase.

Our horses are for our enjoyment, and that may take many forms–it doesn't have to be a competition to see who knows more or who can handle the hottest/fastest/craziest horse.

Aside from checking the horse's attitude and temperament in general, consider that a horse may be seem fine in every respect, but you just don't seem to 'click' with that animal. In that situation I'd keep on looking rather than expect this to change over time. It may, or it may not. I once bought a mare like this. She was easy to handle and ride, and smooth as glass. Though we owned her for five years, I never really *liked* her. Every time I went out to groom the horses I'd suffer guilt pangs because she was definitely last, and least, on my list. No matter how dependable she was, I couldn't bring myself to trust her–and of course this was communicated to her when I rode, which didn't increase my enjoyment of her.

We sold her to an older man, and the two of them have been having a love affair ever since. Always a bit herd-bound and high-strung for me, he takes her out for hours-long solitary rides. Always standoffish with me, she hangs her head on his shoulder and blows in his ear.

She was worth owning, however, because I learned a valuable lesson: don't buy a horse unless you absolutely *love* that animal. Like marriage, you'll be spending a lot of time together and working out any number of problems. It helps if you start out with good chemistry.

Besides the temperamental and emotional matching up, there also should be serious consideration given to what kind of horse will meet your *physical* needs. This is an often sorely overlooked, or misunderstood, point.

As a general rule, the horse you ride should weigh at least five times more than you do. This means if you weight 150 pounds, the horse need only weigh about 750 pounds to carry your weight easily. Most ponies would be quite capable of handling you! If you're a 225 pound rider, look for a horse in the 1100-1200 lb. category. And so on.

There is some variance in this. Most any horse in even moderately soft condition can handle the weights above if not pushed too hard. If the horse is athletic and has a strong conformation—particularly a short back with strong coupling and good bone—chances are it will be able to comfortably carry a significantly greater percentage of its body weight. So if you and your riding gear weigh 300 pounds or more, it's not impossible to find a non-draft horse that can do the job for you. In such a situation it would be best to try the horse out under the conditions similar to those you'll be encountering together to see how he handles it.

One common problem—and I'm guilty of this myself—is choosing a horse that's so tall that mounting becomes a real problem. While I wouldn't rule out a good horse on the basis of height, neither would I go deliberately looking for a very tall horse unless I was a very tall person. Big riders especially are under the misconception that a tall horse is a stronger horse. This isn't necessarily true. A horse with good bone and muscle—especially one with a big strong shoulder and tight coupling at the loins—is more important than one with height. Try not to worry too much about whether the horse will *look* too small for you. If the animal is large and well-muscled, then chances are it won't look too small for you unless perhaps it's a pony. In fact, most ponies can carry a much larger percentage of their body weight than can horses. The diminutive Icelandic Horse is well-known for its weight-bearing and endurance capabilities.

If you end up with a very tall animal, and discover that mounting presents a challenge, then don't be afraid to use whatever resources you need to mount up comfortably. This isn't primarily for your sake, but for the horse's. Too often people are afraid of looking foolish, so rather than using a handy mounting aid or asking for a leg up, they heave themselves onto their hapless animal's back with a big 'thump!' This can lead to worse problems later on, when the horse defends itself by refusing to stand still for mounting.

If you end up with a very tall horse, the best thing you can do to make life pleasant for both of you is teach that animal to stand absolutely still for mounting, no matter where you may ask him to stand. This is a simple lesson that can be taught in an hour. Usually there is a stump, log or slight natural incline that can be inconspicuously utilized for mounting. I've been known to lead my big gelding into a small ditch, and mount him from the edge of that. It's true there are times you may feel rather foolish. But handle it with humor and I'd be willing to wager that over time your good example will encourage others to follow your lead. Many of my regular riding companions have become far less shy about taking advantage of a little 'gitty-up' assistance!

However, when looking for that special horse—all other things being equal—pick the animal that's not too tall for easy mounting.

Riding Evaluation

All right then. You've decided that this horse has the temperament, personality, ground manners and physical attributes to keep you interested. Now it's time to check it out under saddle. Let the current owner/handler mount and ride the horse first, while you watch. Does he stand still for mounting? Walk out without jibbing, prancing, balking or head-tossing? Does he appear attentive to the rider, one ear cocked back to indicate that his attention is on his master? Does he maintain a willing, sweet expression?

Observe the horse at the flat walk, his intermediate gait, and the lope or canter. Does he take up an easy, smooth transition between them? Seem a bit lazy–or too full of himself? If you're going to be doing any road riding, ask the handler to take him near some traffic or farm equipment, so you can observe how he responds to motorized vehicles. This isn't a bad idea in any case, since even trail-riders will run into people on noisy ATV's in the most out-of-the-way spots.

Assuming you haven't observed any behavior to eliminate your prospect from consideration, it's finally time to carefully check out the horse's intermediate gait under saddle. Especially watch the rider, to see how smoothly he sits the gait. There should be little more than a slight, relaxed movement in the riders' back as the horse moves out in a fox trot, running walk, rack or amble. Can the horse come up to a speed comparable to a working trot without continually breaking to a trot or pace? Does it look like the rider has to 'pump' the reins a lot or use an excessive amount of leg and seat aids to get the horse into gait? Does the horse move out swiftly and smoothly while obeying his rider's cues?

It's not hard to determine what gait the horse is performing. In the fox trot the horse moves with its head in a high position, shaking vigorously (as opposed to a deep nod). The hind legs pick up quickly and move upward with noticeable hock action, while the fore legs appear to 'walk' over the ground. This means they are kept low, and there's no moment of suspension–one or the other front foot is touching the ground at all times. The ears may flop up and down at speed, and the tail usually flags.

The horse that racks also moves with a fairly high head, but shakes it less vigorously than the fox trotting horse. When observing this gait, you'll note that opposing front and hind legs (left hind/right fore, then right hind/left fore) will come together in synchrony under the horse. Ideal non-show ring action is smooth, extended and moderately low-slung for good ground-covering action. (The show ring rack is outside the scope of this book, and better left to experienced Saddlebred folks.) There is little head nod or tail shaking.

Some gaited horses tend to slip into a stepping pace, or amble. The pacey horse moves same-side (lateral) legs together, setting the hind foot down an instant before the fore. A horse doing a stepping pace tends to swing its head and body from side to side. Some horses can perform this gait very smoothly. Others are hard to sit. While they don't jar you as much as a trotting horse, the constant back and forth action can make you feel pretty seasick after awhile! Most horses that perform this gait naturally can be conditioned and trained to even it out very nicely. Be aware there are the rare few who will always pace, no matter what you do.

Last but not least, there's the running walk. A horse doing a good running walk has a smooth, loosely rolling action in his shoulders and hind end. His head nods deeply with each step, and his hind foot reaches so far underneath himself that it oversteps the track of the front foot by at least several inches. The head nod and distinct overstep are the hallmarks of a true running walk. A horse performing a good running walk may not even appear to be moving at great speed. In fact, I believe the *best* running walk horses seldom look like they're racing along–it's the length of stride and easy rolling forward motion that gives them such a superb ability to cover ground fast.

Some running-walk horses have the innate ability to perform the gait but have never been ridden or trained in a way to bring it out. It takes a fair amount of good riding to get most Walking Horses to actually 'hit a lick.' You may need to judge such a horse more on his looseness and ability to overstride than on the gait demonstrated during your purchase observation. Sorry to say, many people do not know how to produce, or ride, a good running-walk horse. (You will, with a little reading and lots of practice!)

Now for the lope, or canter. How hard does the rider have to work to get the horse 'gathered' for the canter? Does the horse seem to smoothly spring from its intermediate gait, or a flat walk, into the canter? Does it take the correct lead on a circle, so that the inside front leg seems to be reaching farther out than the outside front? Is it well-balanced, with an even 1-2-3 cadence?

Gaited horses tend to take one or two pacey steps as canter transitions. This is all right so long as the transition is smooth and

Here my daughter Jamie demonstrates a 'Walking Horse canter' on Winston. Note the length of stride. Lateral pairs of legs are slightly more in synchrony than what is common. He could almost be performing an extremely animated and extended walk!

the horse doesn't end up cross-cantering. A cross-cantering horse will be extremely bouncy and poorly balanced. Some gaited horses perform a canter that is slightly more lateral than common. Nevertheless, the gait is still a well-balanced 3-beat canter. Winston, the horse I currently ride, tends toward a lateral motion at the canter–yet it is the smoothest, most well-balanced canter I've ever had the pleasure of experiencing. He also has awesom extension, so that he easily covers as much ground at the canter than most horses do at the gallop. So I don't get too technical about the order of footfalls, but let him do what comes so well and naturally. The important thing is that the canter is controlled, well-balanced and smooth. These qualities make a canter safe and pleasurable to ride.

Many gaited horses, especially those who have a strong tendency to pace, simply cannot perform a good canter. To some people this won't make a bit of difference. In fact, most gaited horse shows have classes for horses that perform only the flat walk and an intermediate gait, with no canter. There are also any number of people who ride the trails, in parades, or simply have fun in their back yards, who never ask their horses to canter.

I recently trail rode with a neighbor who was astride a lovely gray fox trotting horse. We came onto a long level dirt road with no traffic, and I suggested we lope. He looked at me in surprise.

"I've been riding this horse for seven years now," he said, "but I don't even know if he can lope. I've never asked him to before."

Though I was happy to continue on simply gaiting down the road, he decided he wanted to see what his horse would do. So I cued my horse for a lope, and the next thing I knew, my friend and his horse were loping right along beside us. That fellow had no idea what he'd been missing all those years!

The point I want to make is that you need to decide how important the canter is to your riding pleasure. If it's a gait that you seldom or never use, then don't mark your purchase prospect too harshly if it has poor or nonexistent ability to canter. On the other hand if you and your riding friends regularly enjoy a refreshing mile or so of cantering on a regular basis, then you're going to be very unhappy with a horse that simply can't keep up with the other horses, or who consistently cross-canters or stumbles at this gait. You're the only one who can determine the relative importance of a good canter.

If it turns out that your prospect doesn't canter well, and that gait is important to you, don't be tempted to think you can retrain it. Though you might be able to improve its ability somewhat–here's where a working knowledge of conformation comes in handy–chances are it will never canter as smoothly and effortlessly as desired. But take heart. Many gaited horses have a superb 'rocking chair' canter that's second to none. There's always the chance that such a horse will be right around the corner of the next barn you investigate!

Signs of Trouble

There are a few 'trouble flags' specific to the gaited horse industry that you need to beware of during your search for a horse. If you're looking at Walking Horses, check the front pasterns carefully for signs of scarring, rubbed off hair, excess swelling and lumps, or white hair where dark ought to be (which could indicate previous injury or abuse.) Watch the horse very carefully for signs of rear or front foot soreness. By all means drop in to check on the horse at unexpected times—some trainers long used to hiding abuse and unsoundness in this industry will have no trouble fooling you or an unsuspecting veterinarian. If the handler gets unduly upset by this move on to the next prospect, and don't look back.

In any gaited horse, check the hocks for swelling and tenderness. When doing a riding evaluation, ask the horse for a few tight turns around the haunches in each direction to see if it exhibits hock tenderness. Riding downhill will also point this up. Hock problems can be tough to spot, as the symptoms may tend to come and go. Again, check back on the horse more than once before deciding to purchase. This rule is unbreakable—unless you can get a written guarantee of soundness from the seller.

Some gaited horses get what is called a 'slipped patella.' In extremely technical terms, this causes the horse to move with a 'hitch in his gitty-up.' The locked ligament causes him to pick one hind foot up in a very jerky manner. Some surgeries have a limited effect on this—but you should ask if the animal has ever had to have such surgery. Unfortunately, it's often the loosest, nicest moving horses who develop this problem.

One last thing to check for is evidence of forging. A horse with poor coordination and an extremely long stride may hit the back of his front foot or leg with his hind foot. Sometimes the constant banging causes long-term damage to the front limbs. A horse that continually forges may exhibit swelling in the hind cannons as well as wounds that are in various stages of healing. There may also be scarring.

Buying the Young Horse

Maybe you've decided to buy a weanling or horse under the age of two years. If you're an experienced horse person, this can be a fine decision. Otherwise, better to get a well trained older horse. Too many inexperienced horse people have romantic dreams about raising and training their own very young horse.

Photo by Mickey Anderson

The best way to determine the potential of a young horse is by learning about its dam and sire.

Those are the kind of dreams that too often turn into living nightmares.

When choosing a young horse, you cannot necessarily tell by conformation alone how that horse is likely to look and move when it's older. Like all young ones, they tend to grow at different rates so that a horse that looks gangly and a bit sickle-hocked at 18 months of age may be well-muscled with straight legs by the time it's three. Of course you can usually determine essentially what the horse will look like–but there's a greater chance of being fooled.

Because of this, it's a good idea to learn as much about the horse's sire and dam as possible. Check out their conformation, temperament and abilities–especially their ability to gait. This trait is highly heritable, for good or otherwise. A horse that proceeds from two good gaiting parents will almost certainly be a pleasure to ride. If the colt or filly comes from an easily trained, easygoing dam, all the better. It gives you a very good idea about what to expect in the future.

While good riding and training methods may improve any horse, there's never a substitute for good natural gaiting ability, regardless of the horse's age. Avidly look for this, and be determined not to settle for anything less. This alone will dramatically increase your chances of a successful horse purchase.

67

Chapter Four
The Right Start

The best way to ensure your gaited horse will always perform the intermediate gaits correctly is to make sure that horse doesn't get the chance to learn the gaits incorrectly in the first place. This might seem obvious, but incorrect riding, ill-fitting tack or poor handling is the cause of much that goes wrong with our horses–gaited and otherwise. The problem seldom starts with the horse, but rather with it's human handler. The beauty of understanding this is that when we realize that we don't have to fix what has never been broken, we are more likely to take special care to do things right in the first place.

This is simpler than it sounds. Actually, the entire process of getting your horse trained the way you like is not as complex as we tend to make it. I remember when my husband and I planned to have our second child born at home. I went to the library and bookstores and looked and looked and *looked* for information about the actual process of childbirth, and how to be prepared. I was extremely frustrated that there seemed to be so little information out there. The few books available basically taught about warning signs of impending trouble that would indicate we should make a quick trip to the hospital. The only other information they gave seemed absurdly simple: These are the stages of birth, here are the few things you'll need on hand–now relax, and go with the flow! I wondered what was wrong with these people–didn't they realize we were about to undertake an extremely complex and difficult process? After all, childbirth usually requires the services of highly trained and skilled medical personnel. . .I thought that surely there must be more to normal childbirth than simply 'Relax and go with the flow.'

But after successfully giving birth at home I realized this had been, after all, the best possible advice. To tense up and expect problems would have almost surely caused problems that otherwise wouldn't have existed. At the very least it would have made for a tense, unhappy affair–which is what we were trying to avoid in the first place. The best way to make sure there were no unnecessary problems was to relax and let nature take its course. (I want to assure my readers that we *did* have a competent professional assistant on hand–just in case.)

The point here is that it's the same with riding and training our gaited horses. Professional trainers have been in on the act for so long that they've convinced much of the world that their special skills and tactics are necessary. But that's not always true. Usually, the backyard horse lover can do an excellent job of training a horse to move correctly in gait without professional assistance. In fact, most of the time we can do a *better* job of it than do the professionals! There are no special skills needed to qualify you to ride and train a gaited horse yourself–aside from common sense, desire, and good basic riding skills. (We're assuming those who plan to train their own horse already possess these). As with childbirth, the best thing you can do for a good outcome is to simply relax and let nature take its course. This also will help ensure that riding is a pleasurable experience for both you and your horse.

Starting the Young Horse

One of the mistakes we tend to make is to start our young horses working under saddle too hard and too early. This is always a mistake, but perhaps even more so with the gaited horse. Our horse's hocks, especially, are going to be working a bit harder than those of most ungaited horses throughout the animal's life–reaching more, carrying a greater load of weight at certain points of the gait, and taking more steps than a trotter. We need to be absolutely certain that the horse has good, strong mature joints before asking him to do the work of a full-grown horse.

There are two unhappy consequences of starting a horse too young. Right off the bat we're likely to run into what may appear to be 'attitude' problems when the horse starts to balk and refuse our requests. This is often the only means the poor horse has to tell us that he's in pain, and being overworked. Or he may simply not be mentally prepared to 'go to school' full time. Like any immature youngster, his attention span isn't long enough, and he's too easily distracted. Secondly, the animal who's been started too young will break down at an earlier age. So for your sake as well as the horse's, resist the temptation to get your horse started under saddle at too young an age.

How young is too young? That depends. I hate to be too vague about this, but it's much like deciding when a child is ready for kindergarten. Some do quite nicely when they're only four years old. Others can't handle a classroom setting until they're five or six. So it is with our horses. We need to get to know them before we can make an accurate assessment of their training ability.

I've yet to see a horse who's ready for full training under saddle before the age of two years (as in from their foaling date, and not the universal equine birth date of January 1). Some aren't ready until their third year. An immature horse's joints are still too unformed and malleable to handle the stress of training under weight, or working more than a few minutes on a circle. Sometimes an extremely growthy colt will *look* to be ready, because of his size and muscular appearance–but these are often the very ones who need extra time for their bodies' internal structures to fill in as

thoroughly as their outer structures have. Bones, joints and liga-
ments are sometimes under extreme stress just trying to keep up
with the simple daily activities of a horse that's been growing especially fast.

Some people practice 'pushing' a young horse for quick growth
by feeding large quantities of protein rich grain. This may make
the horse stand out in the show ring. This is a poor horse manage-
ment routine. In fact, I'd rather see a horse become a bit thin during a sudden growth spurt than to see one being constantly pushed
to, and past, its limit of growth. Many promising young prospects
are permanently disabled because their joint structures can't tolerate such fast growth. The bones grow faster than the connective
tissues, leading to permanent unsoundness. As with most horse-
related procedures, slow and steady progress is more beneficial in
the long run.

Regarding physical ability and readiness, there's a simple way
to get a fairly accurate idea about whether your horse's bone and
connective structures are strong enough for saddle training. Look
at the animal's front knees. The connective tissue in the knee of a
young horse is still very soft and malleable, making for a bumpy
uneven surface across the front face of the joint. If you feel the
joint, you'll feel an unconnected space of softer tissue on the front
of the joint between the lower leg bone and the upper leg bone.
You'll often, but not always, be able to see this unconnected space.
When the horse's bony structures are mature, this space will completely fill in to form a hard, flat knee bone, covering the joint and
tissues beneath. As a general rule, once the soft tissue has hard-
ened and formed a distinctive knee bone, the horse is physically
ready to begin carrying the weight of a rider. If you begin riding
him more than a few minutes at a stretch before this time, you risk
serious damage to these structures.

If you're unsure about whether your horse is ready for serious
training, consult a veterinarian. Better to spend a few dollars ensuring
the horse's well-being early on than to be stuck with a lifetime of vet
bills brought on by too-early training and resultant tissue damage. To
say nothing of your damaged heart and nervous system.

Many experienced horse people do some very basic under saddle training with their horses at around the fall of their second year, when they're only about 18 months old. This involves a half-hour or so of work each day over the course of about a month. Then the horse is taken out of training until the spring or fall of the next year—or until it shows signs of being mature enough to handle a full training regimen. This practice tends to produce horses who train more calmly than those who are started later. As long as the horse isn't asked to bear too much weight, or worked for too long, there is usually no harm done. The slight risk may be outweighed by the long term benefits to the amateur rider/trainer. You'll have to make this decision for yourself.

The horse's physical preparedness is only one aspect of this question. The other aspect is his mental readiness. A horse that's started too young will not be able to concentrate on his handler long enough—or be able to remember lessons well enough—to make training anything but an exercise in misery. As handlers, there is much that we can to do help get our horses mentally prepared for training.

It helps if this process starts out when the horse is very young—even from birth. Always make sure that when you're handling the horse, he pays attention to you, and respects your personal space. Do not allow nibbling or nipping, or any other kind of 'horse play' that gives the animal an excuse not to pay attention to your commands. Get him used to being haltered, tied, and walking about 2 feet from your side on the end of a lead rope.

Training the Young Horse to Lead

Whether you're working with a young, unspoiled horse or an animal that's been allowed to have its own way at the end of the leadline, it is essential that a horse be taught good leadline manners. Allowing a horse too much freedom while leading will result in more than aggravation and sore toes—it will diminish your position of authority with the animal, and may eventually cause him to challenge you in more serious ways. Also, by teaching your horse to lead properly you are laying important groundwork for more advanced training.

Leadline lessons should begin in the stall or corral, where you begin to establish both your authority, and your personal "respect zone." Place a halter and a shanked leadline on the horse. The chain on the lead must be at least fourteen inches long, as it should cross over the horse's muzzle, through the lower offside ring, and run up to clip on the upper offside halter ring. Carry a longeing whip in your left hand, butt (or heavy) side up. This whip should be unobtrusive, and used only as reinforcement when needed. *Never use a whip to punish a horse*, as this causes fear and defensiveness. A fearful, defensive horse is not a learning horse.

Work in a corner of the enclosure with the animal's off (right) side and butt against the wall. Stand at the horse's near (left) shoulder, facing front. Hold the leadline in your right hand, about twelve inches from the horse's head. This much rope gives the horse enough leeway for natural head motion when he walks, and leaves you enough slack to properly work the lead chain. Coil the excess lead rope in the palm of your hand rather than wrapping it around it, as the latter practice may lead to serious entanglement and injury should the horse suddenly try to jerk free.

Ask the horse to "stand," and insist that he stand in one place, without moving or crowding into you. If the horse tries to crowd you, quickly bring the butt end of the whip up across your chest and jab it into his shoulder as he moves in toward you. Timing here is important, as it should be apparent to the horse that it is his action that causes the discomfort, and not you *per se*. Therefore be ready to jab quickly as the horse moves in toward you. Calmly reposition the horse exactly where he was. Repeat the command "stand," and the lesson, until the horse stops crowding you. This should only take one or two demonstrations. When he realizes that his pushiness consistently causes him discomfort, he'll stop crowding. Praise and pet him when he's standing quietly.

If he tries to walk forward, say "whoa," and stop him by giving a quick jerk on the lead shank and placing the butt end of the whip in front of his chest. Give him a smart thump on the chest

When teaching a horse to lead, work along a wall or fence line. Do not allow the horse to pull ahead of you, but walk about one foot out to its side at the shoulder. Carry a long

whip in your outside hand, held horizontally to the horse's body. Use short snatching motions on the lead line chain to slow the horse down. Bring your arm back and tap him on the hip to encourage forward movement. If he pushes into you you, jab the blunt end of the whip toward his shoulder, so that he punishes himself on it. As you come to a natural obstacle, tell him to "whoa."

with the whip butt if necessary. Once he's standing obediently, give him a pat and word of friendship, and leave the next lesson for another day.

The next time you work with the horse, take the lesson outdoors. Work along a fence line or barn wall. Keeping to the horse's shoulder, ask him to "stand," as before. Once he's doing what is expected, ask him to "walk," and start to move, staying at his shoulder. If the horse lags behind or refuses to move, swing the lash end of the whip behind you, and tap his hock to encourage him along. Some experiment will be necessary to find out how hard this reinforcement needs to be. Some horses jump forward like jackrabbits with the least little tap, others need to be touched with the crop quite firmly before they respond. Start with a very light touch, and increase the pressure as necessary.

If the horse tries to rush ahead of you, give a quick jerk on the leadline to slow him down. Don't keep a steady pressure on the lead chain, trying to pull the horse along, as it will only cause him to pull against you. Allow the horse his head unless he tries to take advantage of you, then use short snatching motions on the lead.

When you reach the end of the fence or wall, give a short snatch on the lead shank and say "whoa." Ideally you will be walking into a fence corner so that the natural barrier will force the horse to comply. If this is impossible, you may need to bring the butt end of your crop up in front of the horse's chest to reinforce the stop command. Use it to give a smart thump on the horse's chest if he tries to ignore even that.

As before, if the horse crowds you, use the butt end of the whip to jab his shoulder. Be matter-of-fact about all this, and keep the lesson moving even during and immediately after a discipline. If you stop work every time the horse misbehaves, you will be rewarding–and thereby encouraging–misbehavior.

The lesson may be somewhat erratic at first, with the horse first rushing ahead, then lagging behind. It will take a short time for you to coordinate your movements with his. But don't worry, you'll both catch on soon enough. Once he starts to understand exactly what it is you want, he'll quickly become more mannerly and consistent. Then it's time to repeat the lesson, switching the leadline around to work from the horse's off (right) side. Don't take any shortcuts, and make certain all lessons are equally reinforced from both sides of the horse.

In a very short time you'll have a safe, obedient horse who is ready to go on to his next lesson. By the way, these lessons can be used to good effect even on an older horse–say one you've just obtained, or one that's grown lazy and needs a little tune-up lesson regarding authority and responsiveness.

Teaching the Horse to Give to Pressure

As anyone who has handled young foals can attest, the natural instinct of a horse is to always move *into* pressure. In other words, if you push on the horse's side, he'll push back. If you pull on his lead rope, he'll resist with every ounce of energy he's got.

This instinct is counterproductive for riding purposes, as we need the horse to learn to *yield* to our pressure aids. The more soft and giving a horse is in this manner, the easier it is to teach him his lessons under saddle. A horse that is stiff and unyielding to his rider will never learn to perform saddle gaits correctly.

So one important pre-saddle lesson we should work on is to teach the horse to step away from pressure–to give at the shoulder, to step sideways when you push lightly at his mid-belly, and to move his hindquarters away from a tap on the hip. These lessons are easily introduced during leadline training, while the horse is being attentive.

Once the horse is leading well, stop her as usual. If you're on the horse's left side, coil the lead line in your right hand, and the training crop in your left. Bring the crop up across your chest, tap the horse on the side of the shoulder with the butt end, and say "step." Keep tapping/requesting until the horse takes a step away from you–then *immediately* stop tapping and praise her for what she's done. Repeat this several times, until the horse immediately understands what you're asking, and responds.

Next lesson, stand farther back, near the horse's midpoint, and use your hand to push at her belly, and say "step." Her initial response will probably be to push back. Reposition her and continue to push with increasing pressure–sometimes a good hard shove or two is in order!–using the "step" command each time, until the horse finally takes a step sideways. Then reward her liberally, and repeat several times until she's got the message.

A word of warning here: it is easy to overdo these simple lessons. I find that often the horse seems not to really understand what I'm asking, but sort of stumbles on the right response once or twice. That's good enough for starts!

Immediately praise the horse and move onto something familiar and easy. Most of the time, the next time I repeat the lesson the horse performs it like an old pro. So don't expect too much the first time you introduce something new, but let the horse know you appreciate her trying. As much as teaching practical skills, you're building a relationship and lines of communication. These will serve you well in the months and years to come. It's more important to maintain good relations than to produce fast results– or to prove who's 'boss.' Treat her firmly, but with kindness, and you won't have to prove anything–she will *know* who's boss. More-over, she'll *like* it that way!

Once the horse has learned to consistently step sideways away from you at your request, ask her to stand, and move out a short distance away from her. If she tries to step toward you, shake the leadline and say 'whoa!" Reposition her if necessary. Repeat this until she's willing to stand quietly while you move about four feet out to her side.

Now use the training crop to reach out and tap her side and say "step." She may step forward or toward you. If so, firmly say "Quit!" (Not "No," since this is too easily confused with "Whoa!" and that should always mean *only one thing*–stop in your tracks *right now*.) Reinforce the command with a shake on the leadline. Reposition her if necessary, and repeat the request until she obeys. It's important that the horse pay attention to you during these early lessons–but have a heart, and when the horse shows signs of wea-rying or becoming bored, cut the lessons short. Sessions should only last from ten to fifteen minute, and be repeated a couple times each week until the horse is ready for more challenging training.

Next, I like to teach my horse to soften and give me her head while I stand at the girth area. To do this, I stand her up square and ask her to stand. Then I ask her to "give," while tugging gently on the leadline. If she moves her entire body, I reposition her and keep on making my request until she bends her neck to give me just her head. (Some cut up bits of carrot hidden in the pocket can be a great incentive in this situation!) Once she understands what I want, I repeat this lesson from the opposite side.

This simple lesson is perhaps one of the most useful training devices we can use on our young horses. In order to resist her rider, a horse has to stiffen it's neck. A horse that has been condi-tioned to soften and bend her neck at a given command will be a horse who can always be brought back under the rider's control. It can prevent balking, bucking and rearing. It can take her mind off

Teaching a horse to bend it's neck softly at your request teaches her basic submission. Start work from the ground, standing at the horse's shoulder. Once she understands and can comply, repeat the lesson from the saddle. (This is later on in training).

'spooks,' and be used to help relax her during stressful situations. This simple training device is one we will repeat often, both from the ground and from the saddle, on young as well as on older horses. It will also be the foundation from which other useful exercises are built from, when we go on to more advanced training.

As to the method of this early training, it ought *always* to be gentle, and positive. Under no circumstances is it advisable to resort to hitting or yelling. These occasions must be fun for both you and your equine friend. If the horse starts putting up too much resistance, back off a step, and ask her to do something that's easy. Then offer lots of patting and praise, and leave it at that. Eventually she'll discover that she likes understanding and obeying your commands. At that point, you've gained an important training ally– the horse, herself!

When the horse is happy to be working with you this way for 15 minutes at a time, you might start longeing lessons–but not before the animal is at least a full yearling. Under no circumstances should a horse less than eighteen months of age be longed for longer than about 5 minutes, and then only at the walk. At this stage, the purpose for longeing is to teach the horse to obey your commands while standing a short distance from you. It's *not* for strengthening the horse–regular outdoors turnout will do that. (Of course you *are* making sure she has several hours of free turnout every day. . .?) Working a horse on a circle is extremely hard on the legs, so when the lessons are going well, don't be tempted into extending them beyond a few minutes to each side.

Once you and the horse have developed a mutually respectful relationship, there's no good reason for continuing to longe regularly until just before saddle training starts in earnest. At that time, it's a good idea to begin longeing to help build muscles while teaching her to round out and relax while being worked. It will also increase her understanding of your voice commands, and reinforce your standing as the 'herd boss', or one to be respected and obeyed. This will help gaited training, specifically, to the extent that a relaxed horse will be in a better physical and mental frame to perform its intermediate gaits correctly. It also prepares a horse for line driving, another important element in the finished horse's education.

You cannot–and should not try–to teach a horse to gait on the longe line (except perhaps to teach him *not* to pace or trot). That's not to say that a naturally loose, gaited colt or filly wouldn't be allowed to gait on the longe line at its own initiative–bravo for the one that does! But this isn't where you *teach* this skill if the horse doesn't exhibit itself spontaneously.

Longeing 101

Our gear for this work is simple: a well-fitted longeing cavesson, a surcingle, longeing crop, heavy cotton or leather gloves, and a 30'-long longe line.

Always wear gloves whenever you longe a horse. If you don't, and your horse tries to pull away, then you risk having to let him go in order to avoid serious rope burns on your hands. If he gets

Early lessons can be strenuous, and the horse may try to pull away. It's important not to lose control. Wear sturdy gloves to protect your hands. Never wrap the lines around your hands, as this could lead to injury if the horse suddenly pulls and runs away. Instead, arrange the line butterfly fashion across your palm, as in this photograph.

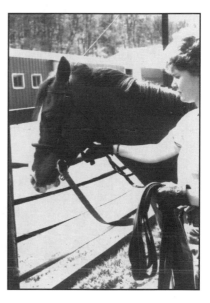

To longe a horse in an O-or-D-ring snaffle: Place the longe line through the bit ring, run under the horse's chin and attach to the ring on the other side.

away with this once, you'll have a real job convincing him to stay on the line next time. I prefer a heavy canvas longe line to nylon, as the former gives me a better gripping surface. Excess line should be folded "butterfly" fashion across the palm of your hand, never looped around it. This way the line can be safely played out, as you need it. Otherwise, if a horse suddenly pulls back and tightens

81

those loops, your hand could be hopelessly tangled in the line–a very dangerous situation with an out-of-control horse.

Some people use a halter for longeing, but a training cavesson or 0-ring snaffle bridle is far better. A horse longed in a halter will soon discover that you have very little control, and will take advantage of this. Also a halter will pull out of place, and could injure the eye.

If you don't want to invest in a training cavesson, then you may safely opt to use a simple snaffle bridle, minus reins, for longeing. This can be beneficial in that it teaches the rudiments of working off a direct (snaffle) bit. Run the end of the longe line through the near side snaffle ring, under the chin, and clip the longe line snap to the off side ring of the bridle.

Work in a 60 foot round ring, if possible. Otherwise you may work in one corner of a larger corral or arena, so you have barriers on at least two sides to work the horse against. If you have no access to such facilities, then rig up a temporary round pen using wooden stakes, rubber hose or even clothesline. A psychological barrier is better than no barrier. A young horse longed in the open is certain to challenge your authority and pull loose, or run wildly out of control on the line.

With a longeing whip in your right hand and the longe line butterflied in your left, situate your horse so that his off side is against the barrier, and tell him to "stand." Facing the horse's shoulder, move backward toward the center of the circle, to a distance of five feet. If he starts to move toward you, repeat the command "stand," snap the longe line as negative reinforcement, and reposition him. If he walks forward, quickly position the butt end of the whip in front of his chest and the command "whoa" to stop him. Be calm and patient.

Once he's standing when you're five feet away, praise him. Now ask him to "walk." Move your body to keep it parallel with the horse's hip. His body should be centered between the longeing whip and the longe line.

In essence, you are leading him in a circle from a distance of five feet. Don't move out any farther! This would put you in range of the back feet, what is known as the dangerous "kill zone." While most horses would never even think of lashing out at their handlers, there is always the possibility–even with the gentlest of creatures–of something unexpectedly spooking the horse and causing him to kick out. Young horses can be very unpredictable, so it's always best to safeguard against every potential danger.

Patiently teach your student to lead in a circle at that five-foot distance. Teach him to stop when you say "whoa," just as you did when teaching him regular leading. Prevent his turning in to face you by using the butt end of the whip at his shoulder to keep him out. If necessary, use the lash end at his hocks to keep him moving forward.

Once you've accomplished all this, end the first day's lesson. In a day or two (no more) repeat the lesson. If he's doing well, switch the longe line and longe whip around to teach him the same lesson from the other side.

After he's moving well in both directions, increase your distance from five to about fifteen feet–always being careful to avoid that dangerous eight-to-ten foot "kill zone." Again, command him to "stand" until you're in position, then ask for the walk. When you're farther away, if the horse tries to face you or move in toward you, use the longeing whip in a sweeping motion across his torso to keep him out and moving forward.

To stop the horse from a distance, drive him into a fence as you ask for a "whoa." In a round pen move in toward his chest and use the butt end of your whip as a barrier. Once he is walking and stopping obediently at a fifteen foot distance, move out even farther and ask for a bit more speed. Use your longeing whip, body language and voice to snap things up. Body language works like this: to slow or stop horse, step in toward his chest; to get him to start moving, or increase speed, swoop your body toward his hip. Don't worry, he'll know what you're asking. This body language is universally understood among equines.

When you ask for speed, all you're asking for is a fast flat walk. While your horse may spontaneously take up a saddle gait, this isn't your goal at this point of training. Whatever you do, don't

To keep the horse moving on the longe line, walk toward his hip. If he tries to pull away, keep toward his back end—but safely out of kicking range. To stop or slow the horse down, move toward his shoulder and point the whip toward his chest. Always longe the horse in an enclosed area.

try to push the horse into gaiting. What you *can* accomplish here, however, is to teach your horse *not* to square trot or pace. If he tends to pick up either gait when you ask for more speed, step toward his shoulder and slow him back down to a walk. Stop him altogether and start over if necessary. *Do not ever allow the horse to pace or square trot on the longe line.* You want to build his muscles for strength, give him a sense of balance, and teach him obedience. But if you allow him to take up an incorrect, lazy-horse gait (which trotting and pacing are for our gaited horses) then you'll be inadvertently training his muscles to 'remember' this incorrect manner of motion. Don't break this rule, and you'll never have to retrain your horse to gait properly.

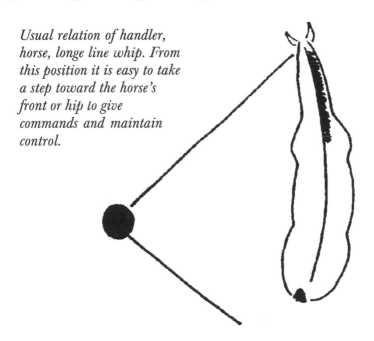

Usual relation of handler, horse, longe line whip. From this position it is easy to take a step toward the horse's front or hip to give commands and maintain control.

Start out with 10-minute longeing sessions, gradually increasing them until you're working together a maximum of 20 minutes. Always work both directions, so that when you're doing full sessions, he's working about ten minutes to each side. Keep calm, be patient with sometimes erratic progress, and end sessions on a good note. If the horse appears confused, back up a step to do something more familiar, and end the lesson there. Remember that no two horses will respond the same, and adapt your methods and expectations to suit the animal you're working with.

Just like you or me, horses have days when things come easy. Then lessons are a pleasure for both of you. They also have days when things seem more difficult, and it's hard to pay attention. Do not tolerate nor encourage laziness or outright rebellion (which may take the passive form of his simply 'tuning you out'), or you'll find him continually testing you. Learn to read his body language– is he being petulant, or frustrated? Rebellious, or bored? If things don't go well for a lesson or two, and you think it's possible he's just having a bad day, give him and yourself a break, and end the training session early. It only takes minutes for one bad experience to shape up–but it can take weeks, months or even years to undo the resulting damage. As a rule it is far better to take things too slow, and give the horse the benefit of the doubt, than to try and rush things along and risk giving him a bad attitude.

Line Driving

Line driving, also known as ground driving, is a training practice whereby you control a horse from the rear by means of two long lines run from both sides of the animal's mouth to your hand. Line driving allows you to acquaint a young horse to new stimuli before work under saddle begins. It helps muscle him up in preparation for saddle work, improves his balance, makes him more sure-footed over varied terrain, and teaches him proper responses to the bridle. It allows him to become desensitized to common, frightful stimuli such as motorized traffic, wind in the trees and the sudden appearance of wild life. Best of all, it builds on and improves the lines of communication and sense of trust between you.

Before line driving begins, the animal must be working correctly on the longe line. He will also need to be accustomed to either a training surcingle or a saddle, and to a snaffle bit. As usual, introduce these things in a relaxed manner, and don't try to hurry the process. With both the surcingle/saddle and the bit I often work with the horse at feeding time, when he can reward himself for not reacting by settling down and eating his grain. Long before I ever place a saddle on his back I've casually rubbed saddle blankets, feed bags, old jackets and whatever else I can lay my hands onto all over his sides and back. By the time we've moved up to a saddle, the horse pays it very little attention.

If he has never carried a bit in his mouth, you should accustom him to it for several days prior to starting him at line driving. Slip a simple D or O ring snaffle–with a nice thick mouthpiece–into his mouth as you offer him a bit of grain, and let him carry it for ten minutes or so. Increase the time he wears it over a couple of nights until he's happy with it in his mouth for a half hour. A horse that is extremely evasive to the bit can often be won over by simply placing a bit of honey or molasses on the mouthpiece.

When you're ready to give him his first line driving lesson, tack up using a surcingle or western saddle. If you use a saddle, hold the stirrups firmly in place by means of a length of twine run through each stirrup and tied under the belly. You'll need two different colored lines, at least twenty-foot long apiece, and a longeing or driving whip. Start work in a 50-60' round pen, or in one corner of a larger enclosure. Wear your gloves. Attach the snap of one line to the right snaffle ring and run the line through the right stirrup or surcingle ring. Rest the coiled right line on the saddle horn or upper surcingle ring, and move over to the horse's left side. Attach the other colored line to the left snaffle ring. Do not run this line through the side ring or stirrup. Holding the left line in your left hand, and while still close in on his left side, take hold of the right side line and carefully lower it along his right side. Moving back to the hip, bring the right hand line around his rump. Move calmly, and firmly pat the horse's flanks and butt as you work so he doesn't get goosey at the unaccustomed feel of the line.

Sometimes a young animal will panic at the feel of the line across his hocks and rump. If this should happen, and he starts to fight vigorously, drop the right side line, move out of harm's way, and control him from the end of the left line by longeing him until he's settled down, just allowing the right hand line to trail along the ground. This is the reason why we don't run the left line through the surcingle ring or stirrup leather right away–it allows direct control from the horse's head, should you need it, and helps avoid snarling the two lines. If a snarl should develop, the different colored lines make them easy to untangle.

You now have one line running from the right side snaffle ring around the horse's rump to your right hand, and another line running directly from the left side snaffle ring to your left hand. Your longeing whip is carried in your right hand.

Now, step back and longe as usual. At first, keep the right hand line quite loose–but don't allow it to hang so low that the horse tangles his hind feet in it. Gradually take up slack in the line

Some Longline Techniques

Prepare the horse for longeing as usual, but run a second line from the offside bit ring around the horse's rump. Use different colored lines on each side to help differentiate between them.

Longe the horse as usual. At first only use the outside line to keep the horse from tipping his head into the circle. Gradually move further to the rear of the horse, keeping equal tension on the lines. Work slowly, giving the horse plenty of time to accustom himself to your new position and the extra line. Once he's working well, move further back yet, and begin to ask him to walk straight forward along a fence line rather than in a circle. Ask for a "whoa" at the corner, and reinforce with the lines. Don't move out of your fenced-in area until he's working quietly and comfortably. Then it's time to begin showing him a little bit more of the world!

Chris McKinney demonstrates another useful longline training technique. She longes the Fox Trotter Wildfire with a come-along on the rump to accustom it to the lines in back (top). Then she attaches a training surcingle, and runs the lines from the cavesson back through the surcingle rings, and longes him this way (center). Finally she moves directly behind him and longlines him around the training pen using the lines for directional control.

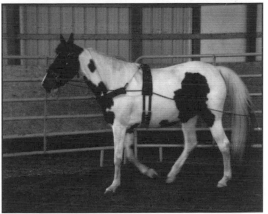

JPhotos by Mickey Anderson

until you've gained control of the animal's right side with the right line. If he tries to tip his nose into the circle, or turn toward you, use the right line (always with a give and take action) to correct him.

Once he's longeing comfortably on a circle with two lines, ask him to lead from both lines along a straight fence or wall while you keep your distance. As you lead him, begin to take a position farther and farther back, until you are finally walking behind the horse (well out of kicking range), controlling him with both lines and driving him forward, when necessary, with voice commands and light popping noises from the whip.

Use your voice to reassure your charge of your continued presence. If at any point he panics and fights, drop the right hand line, move back into a position some distance from the horse's side, and longe him until he settles down. As usual, plan to take this training at a comfortably slow pace, and back up a step or two when needed. Once he's moving happily out ahead of you on the lines, you may quit for the day.

In another day or two (no more), repeat the procedure. When it's apparent that he's comfortable with the new training, you can take the horse out of the enclosed training area, and drive him around new territory. Take him out on the trail, down quiet roads, over bridges and through brush and shallow streams. Walk him over logs, past your neighbor's cow pasture and barking dog, and through simple homemade obstacle courses made up of rubber tires and lengths of lumber.

After he's well balanced (mentally and physically), sure-footed and moving ahead with long forward strides while being line-driven, it's time to teach him to back properly. Stop him in front of a solid obstacle. Now drive him gently "into" the obstacle, and the bit, while refusing to give with your hands. Say the word, "ba-a-ck" very slowly and deliberately. His momentum should be carried backward, instead of forward. Be happy with just a step, or even a rock backward, at first. As he becomes more proficient, teach him as he backs to keep his body straight between the lines.

Line-driving is an important training tool in your horsemanship arsenal. A horse that has plenty of line-driving experience is well prepared to be trained under saddle. Some folks prefer to 'pony' their young stock–that is, to lead them while riding another, more experienced horse. This method has some benefits–most notably that the older horse can lend confidence to the younger horse when he's confronted by new, frightening circumstances. Also of course, it means far less strenuous leg work for the trainer! But in my opinion it also teaches the young horse to depend on the presence of another herd mate, rather than upon his human handler. This kind of dependence can become an outright vice, so that the horse–though well trained in other respects–refuses to ride away from the barn, or other horses. Or else he becomes so determined to keep up with another horse on the trail that he pays little regard to his rider's commands. He panics when separated from his equine buddies and rushes headlong through anything that may separate him from them.

All such circumstances places the rider in a dangerous situation–on top of an excited, out-of-control horse. For these reasons I highly recommend line driving as a more preferable alternative to ponying. Besides all this, you'll reap the benefits of getting lots of good exercise while building a terrific foundation of friendship, understanding and trust with your horse. Both will stand you in good stead when you begin saddle training.

You've accustomed the horse to being handled and obeying basic voice and pressure aids. He's had several weeks of ground driving, and has become confident in situations that used to frighten him. When he has a problem, he's learned to look to you for direction and the confidence to handle it. In short, you understand one another–and he relates to you as a trustworthy master. It's time to ride!

The First Ride

For your first riding lesson, tack up, using an older saddle (I prefer western for the extra sense of security it gives me–but use whatever is most comfortable for you), and prepare as usual for line driving. Take him out and line drive him for 20-30 minutes, until he's nice and relaxed, and not too fresh. Take off the long

Here the rider helps the young horse to keep its balance and understand what's expected by shifting his weight into the turn, and using a leading rein. Young horses need all the physical help you can give when they start to carry a rider. Don't hesitate to use your seat, legs, weight, hands and voice as encouragements.

lines, and attach a pair of clip-on reins to the rings of the snaffle. Stand the horse in a corner of your riding corral, or a corner fence line. It's best if you have a friend who can help you by holding on to his head. Place your foot in the stirrup, tell him very calmly to "stand," and as smoothly and slowly as possible, mount up into the saddle. If he jumps or doubles up to buck while you're mounting, dismount and calm him. Repeat this until he allows you to sit quietly in the saddle.

Chances are excellent, given the working relationship that you've already developed, that your horse will react very little to this new experience. Most of the time the horse simply looks back up at you as if to say, "What in the *world* are you doing up there?"

If your student really gives you a very hard time, and/or if you weigh over 150 pounds, you might consider getting a young, lightweight and experienced rider to give you a hand. That way, you can be the person at the horse's head, calming and reassuring him. Since he's learned to trust you in this manner–and you've learned how to read and respond to him–this method can be quite effective. If he refuses to stand for being mounted, the rider can get on quickly anyway while you control him. You don't want this to turn into a game! As soon as the rider is mounted, you begin to lead the horse around until he's settled down.

Once you're mounted, if you have a friend assisting (this is *really* a good idea. . .), ask her to lead you around the working area for a couple of minutes. Once it seems obvious that the horse has accepted this new experience, have your friend move away and begin to direct him using direct pressure on the reins yourself–just as you did when you were line driving him. If he stops, use your seat and legs to push him forward again. If he refuses to move, use your seat and legs while pulling him into a sharp turn using a direct rein. He'll have to take a step to keep his balance, and then you've got him moving. It won't take long for him to get the idea.

You've now got a genuinely well-started greenbroke horse. The rest, as they say, is just details.

Chapter Five
Lessons from the Saddle

If you've followed the suggestions for early training and groundwork laid out here, you're going to be surprised by how easy–and fun!–saddle work is for you and your young horse. Now you can build a wonderful gaited saddle horse on that firm foundation. Still, the secret to success is patience–and time. Nothing worthwhile is ever completed in a day, or a month. This is especially true with horses.

I'm going to say right up front, however, that at this juncture some of you might simply prefer to turn the horse over to an experienced rider or professional trainer for a month or two of 'wet saddle blankets.' This will be true if you simply don't have time to ride the horse several times a week. The only way to train a horse right is by *frequent and regular riding.* It's also a good idea to get help if you don't feel competent to handle an occasional blow up or hard spook. If riding the horse makes you extremely nervous, this is going to be conveyed to the horse no matter how hard you try to hide it.

If you do decide to hire a trainer, make certain that person knows that this horse is not to be allowed to trot or pace *under any circumstances.* At this point you're not trying to obtain or set a saddle gait, but merely to get the horse used to being ridden, muscled up and confirmed at obeying riding aids. All you want to do is put some miles on the horse–don't expect him to be 'finished.' Many trainers are so accustomed to customer who insist on having a 'wonder horse' produced in 30 or 60 days, that you'll have to convince them that is *not* your desire. This is the primary problem with using a trainer–all they really know are unwise training techniques and devices they've learned to employ in order to turn out horses as quickly as possible. (For this reason, I prefer a dressage barn. These trainers are usually glad to take the necessary time to work on basics.)

If you use a trainer, go often to watch the horse being worked, and make opportunities to ride the horse during this time yourself. If something doesn't seem quite right, get your horse out of that barn as quickly as possible. Don't doubt your instincts for one minute! One bad training experience can undo in a day what you've been building up over the horse's lifetime.

When I've got a horse that challenges my level of competence–I'm certainly no cowboy–I invite a friend who's an extremely accomplished horse woman to come trail riding with me

The first few times out under saddle, riding with an older, more experienced friend can help calm an inexperienced horse (and nervous rider).

Photo by Mickey Anderson

For the first few rides, it helps to use very gentle, easy-to-understand aids for the horse. A leading rein is useful not only to cue for a turn, but also to encourage your mount to take a step if he hesitates to do so. This is much preferable to banging on the horse's side with your boots!

and the young horse for several days. At first she rides the young horse while I ride an older mount to which he's accustomed. After a few days, we switch mounts. This has worked not only with young horses, but with the occasional problem horse I've had to deal with. In return, I sometimes go to her place and ride one of the horses that she's started, just to put some miles—and perhaps a little polish—on him. We all have our stronger and weaker suites, and it is to our, and the horse's, benefit to understand what they are and work accordingly.

After your first time up in the saddle, it's a good idea to spend another few days in a safe, enclosed place, getting the young horse used to balancing a rider and recognizing basic riding cues from someone sitting directly on top of him. This includes pushing him forward using your seat and legs and stopping him with a light touch of the reins, your tensed seat, and a soft "whoa." At first use a leading rein, but since he's become accustomed to responding to a direct rein while being ground driven, you should be able to use a direct rein within a day or two. Be very consistent in using *all* of these aids, so that when the time comes to eliminate the voice aid he won't become confused. (You don't want someone else's horse responding to *your* spoken voice aids now, do you?)

Once you've accomplished these things–which may be a matter of minutes, but will be fully integrated into his understanding within a few days–you should take him out on an easy trail ride. If you've been ground driving him alone, there's no reason to expect this will be any different. In fact, you might even saddle him up and ground drive him for a half-hour or so on the trails to warm him up and calm him down, then switch from long lines to reins, mount up, and ride the horse home. If he's a high-strung horse that will try to rush toward home, ride him out, and long line him home. If the prospect of riding alone the first time makes you a bit nervous–or if he's by nature a more nervous, spooky individual–then invite a friend with a familiar, steady older mount to come along.

It's a good idea at this stage to give the horse as much variety as you can. Work him in the arena, then take him out on the trail. Expose him to road riding–assuming you've accustomed him to traffic during your long lining training. Take him out on some deserted dirt roads, and let him move right out. Trailer him over to a local show, and long line him around the grounds. Then work him in a practice arena. The more riding, and the greater amount of variety, the better.

At least twice a week, however, you should be doing some arena work with the horse. This will help you work on skills that advance the horse's training while preparing him mentally and physically to perform his gaits under saddle. An enclosed arena or paddock helps to ensure that the horse doesn't become too distracted by nearby sights and sounds, but an empty flat pasture that has a gate between it and the barn will do the trick when necessary. Don't think you can neglect this last requirement. A young horse that thinks it can run to directly to the barn will not be giving you it's full attention–and may catch you off guard. Don't give it the opportunity.

For a young horse, variety is more than just the spice of life—it should be the main ingredient! The more experiences you expose the animal to, the more useful and trustworthy he will become. Ride the young student on country roads (top), through woods and streams (center), and around local show grounds. Do not allow him to do anything but **walk, walk, walk** *on these forays. It doesn't matter if he can't yet walk* **fast**—*speed will come eventually. For now your goal is to get him seasoned and muscled up. If you allow the horse to trot or pace, he will be learning the wrong lessons and building the wrong set of muscles.*

Photos by Mickey Anderson

Not Just for Kids

The exercises that follow are not just for young horses. They are extremely useful for horses of all ages. If you take a horse at any stage of training and put him through these exercise regiment, I guarantee you'll have a better riding horse within a few short weeks. In a couple of months the improvement in the horse–and your level of enjoyment–will be remarkable.

These exercises help build the horse's stamina, teach him to shorten and lengthen his stride, reinforce obedience to the rider, make him light to your riding aids, and cause his body to become strong, yet relaxed, soft and supple. You should know that they are really nothing more than basic dressage moves. Many of you may be turned off or intimidated by the dreaded 'D' word. I know I used to be. We tend to picture high-class riding stables, expensive warmblood horses, and joyless routine riding. While it's true that some of this work involves repetition, that doesn't have to mean the same thing as 'boring.' When we're challenged, we're seldom bored. The same is true of our horses. And dressage work is our challenge to ourselves and our horses to improve both physical and mental abilities on a day by day basis. Few things are more exciting than taking a strung-out, nervous young horse through his paces until we've helped to produce a responsive, confident and well-balanced riding mount.

Don't worry too much about getting every 't' crossed and 'i' dotted when doing these exercises. You're not trying to win a dressage competition, and if you're reasonably careful to go through the exercises as described, you'll get the results you're after.

Take yourself and your horse through these exercises, and I guarantee you'll produce a significantly better riding horse than if you decide to simply ride the trails as a passenger on a horse that knows little more than how to go forward and–maybe–backward. I also guarantee that your horse will be smoother-gaited than he will be if you decide to skip them!

Start these exercises by encouraging your horse to bend its neck to develop flexibility and softness under saddle. A soft horse is much less resistant to riding aids.

Exercise One: Bending the Neck

This exercise is simply a mounted version of the neck exercise given in chapter four. In fact, before you mount, you should ask the horse to give his head to you once or twice from each side. This will prepare him for the request while you're in the saddle.

Mount up and place your right hand about a foot down farther on the rein than usual while leaving the left rein totally slack. With direct 'give and take' tugs on the right rein, ask the horse to bend his head back toward your riding boot. Reward him when he obeys, and then ask him to do the same thing from the opposite side. Repeat this to each side two or three times.

Exercise Two: Teaching the Horse to Bend

This might sound absurd, but the truth is all horses travel crookedly until they've been trained to travel with their bodies in a straight line. You wonder, 'So what?' One of the golden rules of riding is that the rider's goal is to 'keep the horse between the seat and hands.' In other words, all of his energy is 'caught' between the impulsion created by your seat and legs and the check of that impulsion through the bit. This makes the horse's frame somewhat like a loaded spring action device. A horse that's traveling in a crooked frame is a horse that's poorly connected to his rider's aids–hands, legs and seat. His energy, rather than being 'caught,' sort of 'leaks out' in all directions. He has little or no impulsion from behind–which is what makes for a smooth ride.

Another condition that will cause stiff, uncomfortable gaits is a horse with flat, resistant stiff muscles. Some horses are more inclined toward this–and these often possess a strong tendency to pace. The cure for this is to teach the horse to soften, flex and bend.

It will be impossible to get a crooked or stiff horse to correctly round out his frame to perform his gaits well. His improperly used muscles will tend to make him one-sided, causing him discomfort when asked to move or bend in a certain way. An

*The mare below is stiff from head to tail. Note the sharp angle at her poll. It's not coincidental that she has a **very** strong tendency to pace. She actually benefited greatly from the exercises outlined in this book.*

Horses tend to naturally move in a crooked frame. This causes their muscles to develop in a lopsided manner. Under saddle, a crooked horse is impossible to collect and round out. All its energy tends to 'leak' out, causing it to move in a strung-out, inefficient way.

Compare this horse's lovely soft, developed frame with that of the mare on the opposite page. They actually have similar conformations—this horse is the goal!

Photo by Mickey Anderson

uncomfortable horse is often an uncooperative horse. I think you get the message: Straight horse is good, crooked horse is bad.

The purpose of this exercise is to teach the horse to travel straight, while remaining soft, light and supple to his rider's cues. And how do we teach the horse to go straight? By teaching him to bend! A horse that can easily bend around his rider's leg is one with soft, giving muscles that can also obey the rider's cues to go straight.

For this exercise, set out two traffic cones, painted milk jugs, plastic crates, or anything else that can be used as visual cues. Place them at about a 60 foot distance from one another. Ride the horse around these cones in a figure 8, being especially conscientious to use correct riding aids as you ask the horse to move forward, bend and turn. Use a direct rein and–perhaps most importantly–both legs. Don't get lazy and do zig-zaggy circles, but try to do a consistently round circle at each end of the figure eight, crossing at the same center point each time.

When you ask the horse for a turn to the left, keep your left leg steady on him right at the girth. Bring your right–or outside–

Aids for bending the horse. The outside leg (dark spot) comes behind the girth and actively pushes the horse's loins to keep them from drifting out of the circle. The inside leg (white spot) is held steady at the girth. A direct rein is applied to the inside rein, while the outside rein is simply held steady. At left are aids for turn to the right, turn to the right illustrated at left.

Riding simple figure eights can work wonders for your horse's physical ability to perform smooth gaits.

Chris is using both reins and her legs to communicate to her horse.

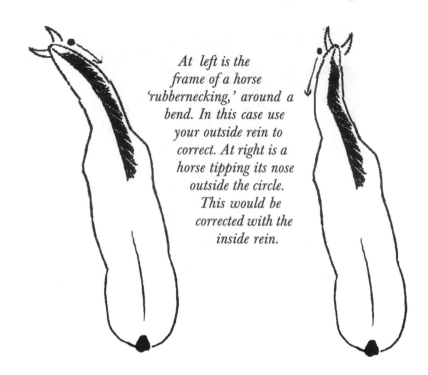

At left is the frame of a horse 'rubbernecking,' around a bend. In this case use your outside rein to correct. At right is a horse tipping its nose outside the circle. This would be corrected with the inside rein.

leg slightly back, and use it in a light tapping way to 'push' the horse around the turn. Use as much energy with this leg as necessary, and no more. This helps teach him not to turn using only his neck, while swinging his hind end out in a wide arc. In effect, he's bending his body around your left, or inside, leg. This sequence is reversed for a turn to the right.

The horse should be encouraged with seat, legs and hands to keep his head and neck in a smooth arc with his body, not poking it outside the natural curve of the turn, nor dropping his nose down so that it's traveling inside the curve of the turn. As he rounds the cone, if he tends to nose out of the circle, use your reins to encourage him to bring his head and neck back into the correct frame. If his neck bends too much so that his head drops and he's rubbernecking around the turn, use your outside rein to correct him while giving a slight lift on your inside rein to lift his head. Your primary goal here is to get the horse to round out and flex laterally (from side to side), so that he's moving more like a thin band of curved aluminum than a slab of wood. At the same time you want to avoid having him learn to 'rubberneck' around the turns, while the rest of his body swings wide, like a semi-truck. It may take a couple of weeks to get good consistent results, but it's well worth the effort. You'll both see and feel the difference, once it comes!

While performing these exercises it's a good idea to mix things up a bit so that neither you nor your horse get bored. Occasionally change direction, take a break from the figure eight and circle the arena, ask the horse for a stop, or a bit more or less speed. Remember to reward him promptly and liberally when you feel him loosening up and performing the exercise willingly and correctly, without any hesitation at the turns.

Once the horse is moving in a smooth, balanced fashion, and can be maneuvered using your body aids, it will be easy to correct him and set his frame up properly when he moves crookedly.

Exercise Three: The Rein Back

Backing lessons should not be performed until the horse is consistently and willingly moving energetically forward an a loose rein. If you start these lessons too soon, you may be teaching your horse how to evade work! So be sure your horse is enjoying the work you do together before starting these exercises.

The rein back is nothing more than backing up–correctly. Many people think that backing a horse consists of simply pulling the reins until the horse starts moving backwards to avoid the pull on his mouth. Not so. When we back a horse what we're doing is generating forward energy, and then checking that energy with our reins so that it carries him backward rather than forward.

Start your horse out at an energetic walk, and keep him moving until he's loose and relaxed. Then stop him in front of a fence or other solid barricade. Use your seatbones and legs at both sides to ask the horse to 'go' with your body. As he rocks forward, check him evenly with both hands–don't *tug* at the bit, but rather keep a short rein and refuse to soften your hands and give. At the same time, say "ba-a-ack." If he tries to turn, set him up again and repeat the exercise. If necessary, enlist the aid of a friend, and have that person lightly push at the horse's front shoulder to reinforce your aids. (Aren't you glad you taught him to move away from pressure?) Immediately–as soon as he so much as rocks back a little–praise him for a job well done and go on to something else. Repeat this exercise until the horse is backing up for as many steps as you ask. Use your leg and rein aids to keep him backing straight.

After the horse has backed up for his last step, always press him forward so that he comes back *on* to the bit and stops in a balanced frame, with his weight evenly distributed among all four legs.

Exercise Four: Half Halt

The next exercise is to help your horse learn to collect his energy so that it can then be directed in a certain direction or fashion. It also helps to teach him to 'listen up,' or 'pay attention because I'm about to ask you to do something.' As the horse is moving energetically forward, begin to ask him for a 'halt' with your seat and hands. (You do this by slightly stiffening your seat bones and not moving them with the horse, and at the same time holding, or checking, his forward motion with the reins.) Pay close attention now, for the very *instant* that he starts to slow down, you need to push him forward again with your legs and seat.

The result of this move is that the horse shifts his weight more toward the rear. His center of balance is then moved backward, and he becomes, in a manner of speaking, 'coiled to strike.' He's light and ready to be asked for a change of gait, a turn, or anything else that you may request.

Frequent half-halts during riding exercises–or any time that you're on the horse–is an excellent device for teaching a horse how to travel in a light, balanced and collected fashion, while paying close attention to his riders cues. I recommend that they be performed regularly when you're riding–even on the trail.

Exercise Five: Head Lowering and Neck Stretching

The following work will help prepare your horse to learn to collect. If you've been using a bosal, it's time to switch to a simple snaffle bit. After the horse has loosened up with some easy circles and figure eights, lower your hands to about wither height on either side. With light intermittent tugs to one side and then the other, encourage the horse to lower and stretch her neck and bring her nose down low. As her head starts to lower to meet the bit, lengthen your reins to encourage her to lower it even more. If you've ever watched western pleasure riders working their horses for the show ring, you've seen plenty of this 'lowering the head' work! When your horse's head is reasonably low, and she will travel along this way, reward her by letting her mouth just 'meet' the bit. Then–ever so slowly and slightly– begin to bring your hands back up and shorten the reins, giving light rhythmic tugs on the reins, so that she yields to the bit and rounds at the poll. Don't expect to get her truly collected at this point–that's not your goal. You simply want to teach her to relax, stretch and then flex her neck so that she will be *able* to collect when the time comes. A little progress each day is all you can expect, but this will add up to a substantial improvement over a week or two.

Exercise Six: Achieving True Collection

Once the horse has had several weeks of exercise, and is easily bending and stretching, lowering and raising her head, it's time to teach her collection. This will enable her to work off the strength and energy of her hindquarters, and move in a soft, rounded frame. One very real benefit of this is that collected horses simply don't pace.

Begin by doing the neck lowering exercises, above. Then use your legs to push the horse forward while asking her to lift her head and round out at the poll. Work at a brisk flat walk. Once she's responding to you by rounding up and becoming lighter on the bit, immediately allow her to relax and stretch out again. Don't work her at collection for more than a few minutes at a time. Rather, ask for collection, and then encourage her to relax and stretch back out. This work will do her a *world* of good.

Too low. . .

Achieving true collection can be a challenge, as horses find many ways to evade the very real work of exercise. The rider here is working with a horse who has overflexed at the poll, getting behind the bit.

Too high. . .

This mare is in front of the bit, with her head held high and back hollow.

Just right. . .

Persistent work pays off as the horse from the center photo demonstrates a soft frame and true collection.

Be careful not to pull on the horse's mouth, or the work you do will be counterproductive. A horse that's resisting too much pressure on the mouth raises it's head, shortens stride, disengages the hocks, and hollows it's back. When asked for more speed, it will most likely break to a trot or pace.

Exercise Seven: Lengthening and Shortening Stride

Now we're starting to get into work that will have a direct bearing on your ability to teach the horse how to perform correct saddle gaits. In truth, the basis of most saddle gaits is a fast, extended walk. If you teach the horse to collect and extend it's stride on demand, then simply encourage it to extend it's stride *and* increase speed, without changing gaits–then you've taught it how to gait. Most horses will pick up speed when asked to–training it to maintain a walking gait and lengthen stride *instead* of merely switching to a trot or pace while increasing speed is our first challenge.

These first exercises can be performed as easily on the trail as in the arena, provided you have smooth, easy terrain. While moving forward at an energetic walk, gently ask the horse to collect.

111

At left is a horse as it might move across a field. There is no impulsion generated from behind. He just drags himself across the ground. (Some non-gaited breeds' 'Western Pleasure' show divisions encourage this type of movement!)

Left entirely to his own devices under saddle, this drawing shows how a horse might move. His head has picked up, and there's a little more energy in his movement—but overall he's still not in a good active working frame.

Then perform a couple of half-halts to get the horse gathered for action. Once he is, lean *very* slightly back in the saddle and energetically press the horse forward with your seat and legs while moving your hands in an easy 'give and take' action on the reins, in close synchrony with the horse's head and neck motion. While you won't be actually 'pumping' the horse's head, your shoulders will be rolling and each arm moving vigorously to keep time with the forward stretching action of his neck. If he breaks into a trot or pace, bring him immediately back down, then repeat the above sequence. You want the horse to increase the length of his stride, but not to break out of a walking gait. You'll know you've got it when you feel like you're *rolling* across the countryside in an even, fast walking gait.

As we correctly ask the horse to shorten his stride, his frame condenses, and his hocks engage. This produces smoother, more synchronized energetic motion.

When we correctly ask the horse to lengthen stride, he maintains energy (impulsion) and synchronization. This is expressed through more forward motion via a longer stride.

It's especially important in this exercise not to hinder the stretching and bobbing action of the horse's neck and head, or you'll be creating tension throughout the horse's body that will be counterproductive to your goals. You must have soft, supple hands and good seat balance to make this work. Otherwise you risk doing more harm than good.

To shorten his stride, begin to slightly stiffen your arms and hands–don't pull on his mouth, but don't give him quite so much latitude as you have been. At the same time, make your legs and seat a bit more inactive–not passive, but just not pushing the horse as vigorously forward as before. You'll know you've met success when the action of the walk feels essentially the same–regular and with good impulsion–but you're going at a noticeably slower pace.

Shortening and lengthening stride is an exercise that can be performed frequently when you're riding, just to keep the horse on his toes. A wonderful benefit of this exercise is that it enables him to stretch and flex along his topline. This is a prerequisite for any kind of smooth saddle gait.

Exercise Eight: Cavalletti Work

This work can be a lot of fun, and is of great benefit for both horse and rider. It teaches and conditions the horse to stretch the muscles along his topline, to pick up his feet, and to shorten and lengthen stride. It also improves balance for both horse and rider. However, if not performed carefully it will also tend to encourage trotting–so don't do this work at speed, or over raised poles, unless you're trying to cure a horse of pacing (see chapter six).

Start by laying a 6' long pole on the ground, and walk over it, leading your horse. Then mount, and ask him to ride over the pole. Give a little leg pressure as he comes upon the pole, to encourage him to pick up his feet. If he knocks the pole with his feet, give a little verbal reprimand–I always say, "pick them up!"

When he can cross the pole without hitting it, it's time to add another one. Lay this one approximately one average stride length away from the first. You'll need to experiment to find the length that works best. As a rule it will be somewhere between 3-1/2' and 4-1/2'. Ask him to walk over them, again encouraging him not to touch the poles with his feet. Add a third pole at the same distance, and repeat.

Once he's crossing these satisfactorily, on the other side of your work area place another three poles, these about a foot farther apart than the first three. Ride him around the arena, first over the short-strided set of poles, and then around to the longer-strided set of poles. In between, ask him to lengthen/shorten his stride. It may take some time, but before long your horse should be able to naturally shorten and lengthen his stride between the two sets of poles, and cross them without hitting his feet on any of them.

This work is deceptively simple, as regular cavalletti work can help you to accomplish a great deal in a relatively short span of time.

Exercise Nine: Lateral Work

These exercises are also extremely useful ones for the gaited horse, as they teach him to yield his body laterally to his rider. When you're working at getting the horse to gait properly, there may be times when you'll ask your horse to respond to a lateral riding aid in order to 'break up' the timing of an incorrect gait. In other words, you'll want him to 'give' just one half of his body, front or back, while holding the other side steady. Don't attempt these riding routines with a very green horse. He should have had a few months of regular riding, bending and circling, before being asked to do lateral work. Even then, don't expect perfection right away. These exercises are tougher than they appear.

The first exercise to work on is the 'shoulder in.' Ride the horse down the side of your arena or work area. Using one rein, tip his nose into the center of the arena until you can see his eye. Walk him around the arena this way, letting him unbend and walk normally at the corners. Turn and ask the same from the other direction, to the opposite side.

When he's become used to this, ask him to bend his neck a little more. Use your outside (close to the rail) leg a bit behind the girth to keep him from swinging his haunches out in that direction, while pushing him forward with your inside leg. Remember it's only the neck you want turned to the inside, and not the horse's entire front end. Also use your leg and rein to correct him if the horse tends to 'drop' his inside shoulder lower then the outside shoulder–a person on the ground can tell you if he's using this common way to avoid the work of stretching and bending.

Next I suggest a simple 'haunches in' or 'double tracking' exercise. Start by working the horse to the right. Walk your horse several times around your arena or work area, using your seat and legs to create good impulsion, or energy from the rear. Keep a soft, regular contact on the bit. When he's moving in an easy, energetic but relaxed fashion, take him down a center line in your work area, and perform a half-halt or two to get his attention and increase collection.

*This illustrates correct riding aids for the shoulder in (to the left). Remember it's the shoulder you want to affect—you want to be riding in a straight line with the horse's nose tipped to the inside of the arena. Only work at this a few minutes at a time to start—it's **very** hard work for bothhorse and rider. If overdone, it will lead to stiffness rather than softening up.*

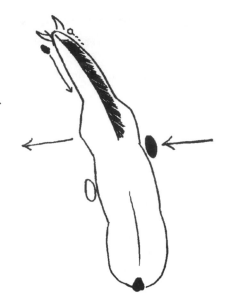

The correct riding aids for haunches in, or two-tracking, exercises. You want the horse to 'give' the back end of his body, so that he's moving on separate tracks, front to back. Again, you'll be moving in a straight line down the arena.

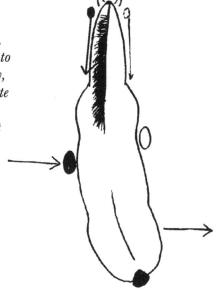

As soon as he's shifted his weight slightly back, and you've moved him energetically forward from there, take a slightly stronger hold on the reins. Don't hold the reins real tight, just don't be quite as soft and giving with your hands. Now move your left leg behind the girth, and use it to tap the horse's haunches off track, to the right. For a green horse, this might mean giving a good thump once or twice, until he gets the message. You want the horse's left hind foot to track where his right front foot has been. Some folks would call this 'dog walking,' as the horse is literally moving on two tracks, the way dogs commonly do. Your right leg is at the girth, being very passive. Your left leg is behind the girth, being very active.

If the horse tries to stop, use both legs and your sliding seat bones to push him forward–give a little 'cluck' if necessary. If he tries to turn to the right in response to what he's learned is 'outside leg pressure,' steady and keep his body straight using both reins, with stronger pressure on the left rein.

Keep the pressure on with your left leg and seat until you feel him 'give,' and move a step or two with the back end of his body out of alignment with the front end of his body. As soon as he does so, release all pressure and ask him to relax and keep moving forward in a regular straight fashion. After he's relaxed, ask him to perform the movement again.

Your goal is to get the horse to move on two tracks, with his body straight beneath you. Practice this exercise until the horse immediately gives his haunches to your leg–and then stop immediately. Don't overdo these exercises, as they are very hard on the horse. Reverse the sequence and ask him to move his haunches to the left by pressing with your seat and right leg behind the girth. Chances are, you and the horse are going to stiffen up when you first try these exercises. But like most things, they'll come easier with time and practice. Each time he performs a few steps correctly, straighten him out and get him to move forward easily and lightly. Within a few weeks you should be able to ask your horse to double track to either side for the entire length of your arena.

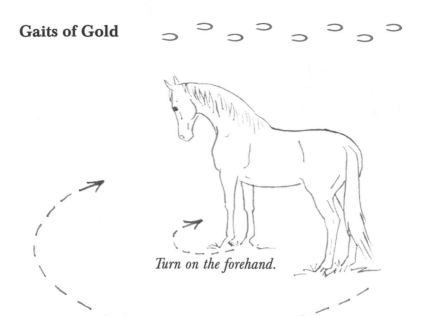

Turn on the forehand.

Exercise Ten: Turn on the Forehand

Now that the horse has learned to yield his haunches to your riding aids, it's time to teach him to take this one step further and teach him to do a correct turn on the forehand. What this means is that the horse will walk his hind end entirely around in a circle while keeping his front end in the same place, moving only one front foot and pivoting–or perhaps describing a small circle–with the other. Again, this is excellent groundwork for teaching the horse to 'give' laterally to your riding aids.

Start this exercise by asking the horse to double track to the right. As he's moving forward, give less and less with your reins, but keep pressing very firmly with your right foot behind the girth. What you're doing is asking him to stop in front and keep moving–but to the left–behind. With an active seat and legs, you're encouraging the horse to maintain impulsion, so that he performs the movement correctly. You don't want to simply start from a standstill, so that the horse does a static, backward movement with no energy or impulsion. All action should be performed with *energy*, or impulsion, from behind.

The Missouri Fox Trotter stallion, King Midas, being taught a reining horse spin. In this photo he's still working on a direct rein, performing a simple turn on the haunches. The next step was to teach him to work off a neck rein, and at speed.

When the horse has stopped his front end, and taken a stop or two to the left with his hind, praise him liberally. Get him to relax, and then repeat the exercise. This is one exercise that I like to have down pat before repeating it to the other side–so you will probably be working only to get your horse to move his hind quarters to the left for a couple of days. Ask for a few more steps each time the exercise is repeated, until he's walking his hind quarters entirely around his forehand. Once he's working well in one direction, teach him to perform the movement going the other way.

Exercise Eleven: Spiral/Turn on Haunches

Once your horse is easily bending and turning, collecting and stretching, using a low, direct rein and your outside leg behind the girth, ride it in an ever-decreasing spiral until it's turning around it's own haunches. Push it into a swift flat walk around the arena before repeating this exercise to the opposite side. After you've practiced this to each side for several days, you may find your horse naturally performing a very nice, even rack or running walk after coming out of the spiral!

You should practice this with the goal of teaching your horse to perform the spiral on a neck rein. Once he's tightened up the circle enough, you'll have him performing a true turn on the haunches–i.e.: he will be setting one hind foot and circling his front end around his back end. Learn to perform this with enough ease and speed, and you'll have the beginnings of a good reining horse spin!

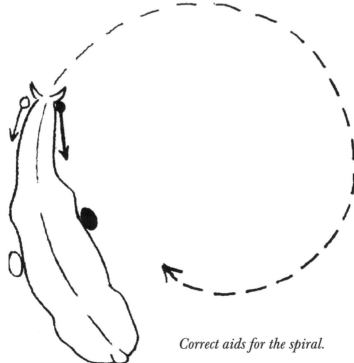

Correct aids for the spiral.

Exercise Eleven: Side Passing

Side passing is one of those moves that will impress the dickens out of everyone, is extremely useful–and not difficult to teach.

Start out the same way that you would if you were preparing to perform a double-track exercise. Instead of moving your active foot behind the girth, keep it *at* the girth, and use it to press the horse's body sideways. Tap and press with as much vigor as you need to get him to move away from the pressure. Keep his front end steady with both reins, to keep him from dropping a shoulder or bending his neck as though to turn. (This allows all that energy you're creating with your seat and legs to 'escape,' and makes the move more difficult for the horse.) What you're asking the horse to do is to move both sideways and forward at the same time. Work with him on this until he's get it down pat, both directions.

Now that he's moving forward and sideways, we have only to generate plenty of forward impulsion but direct more it sideways, until he's moving entirely off your leg, to the side. You do this by simply using the rein to hold him back more and more, and your leg to push him to the side. It can help, when you're

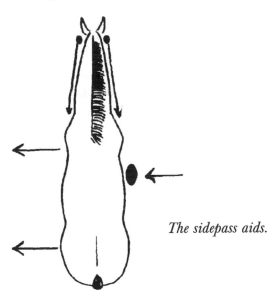

The sidepass aids.

ready for a straight sidepass with no forward steps, to stand the horse in the corner of a fence line so that stepping forward becomes impossible. We need to do whatever we can to make it easy for our horse to understand and obey, and hard to disobey.

With all of the above exercises, you'll start out by giving the horse very strong and direct aids–using legs, seat, hands and even voice when necessary. As time goes on, the aids should become more and more subtle, so that eventually only you and the horse will know what you did to cause him to do what he did. After awhile these moves will become so subtle and second-nature that even *you* may have difficulty explaining to someone how you do what you do with that remarkably well-trained horse of yours!

Gait Training

At some point during these early lessons you will begin to ask the horse to perform his natural intermediate gait. It's impossible for me to tell you what the 'ideal' time for this may be. Some horses will be naturally gaiting from the first day you ride–it will be hard to get them to slow down *out* of gait to perform training exercises. Others won't be ready for several weeks, or months. It's not unusual to get a young horse started under saddle one year, and then to encourage him to fast gait the following season, after he's had a year of training and growth.

Usually the transition from the flat walk to gaiting is nothing more than asking for increasingly greater speed and longer stride. You'll know the horse is ready for this when he is very at ease, soft, supple and well-balanced under saddle. If you start asking for gait before this time, he'll learn to tighten up and hollow out his body. This will lead to his becoming a tense, poorly balanced horse. Not a good idea.

When you believe the horse is ready for gait training, place him into a simple curb bit, with about a 5" shank. This will help him to flex and round out in a manner more conducive to a fast riding gait. Ride him for a few days in this bit, taking him through your usual routines, before asking for gait. When you begin this work it helps if you have an experienced ground person to work with. This person can check to make sure the horse is moving in correct form so you won't risk getting the horse established in improper gait or body frame, and then have to go back later to correct it. It's much easier to get the horse started right in the first place than it is to correct early mistakes.

Walk to Fox Trot

For a fox trot, ask for increased stride and slightly (and I do mean *slightly*) pick up his head with the reins. This helps to free up his shoulder for more extended forelimb reach. While his nose will be definitely above the vertical, your goal is most definitely *not to* get him moving forward with his nose high in the air, stargazing.

When he goes into gait, you will feel his center of gravity shift slightly to the rear. The gait might feel just a bit 'choppy' behind right at first. As long as the horse's isn't doing a square, flat

King Midas at the fox trot.

123

trot, don't worry about this. He'll become smooth and rhythmic with practice. As he becomes accustomed to working in gait–this means hours of work, preferably in a nice outdoors environment over varied terrain–you can ask for more and more speed. Avoid, however, just asking for more speed all the time. As with the walk, you should be asking for shortened and lengthened stride, and for various speed transitions within the gait. You'll also be bringing him back into the bridle, a little bit at a time so that he flexes at the poll.

Once your horse becomes set in his gait, you'll feel the rhythm becoming more even. There will be a light springy feel to the action. His head will shake vigorously, and his ears will keep time–maybe even with vigorous flopping! While action will be obvious throughout your horse's body, *your* body will hardly feel a thing. You'll get the distinct impression that your horse *loves* moving out this way–because most of them really *do*. It's what they've been bred for.

If the horse tries to go into a trot or pace, rather than fox trot, bring it back to the walk and start over. Some horses will fox trot right off the bat, others require more patience. If the horse consistently trots or paces, you may need to try some of the remedies suggested in chapter 6, or experiment with shoeing and bitting. Chapter seven will help get you started in this. It's important, however, not to jump to a new method too quickly. Try one thing for several days before deciding that it won't work and trying something else. Better to have slow progress than a totally confused horse.

The Amble

The amble is a lateral gait. Performed correctly, it can be very comfortable. It's also easy on the horse. Horses that prefer to pace can usually–though not always–be trained to execute a nice amble instead. In fact, that is the primary purpose for teaching the amble. As a rule, if your horse tends to trot you'll train him to a fox trot, rack or running walk. If he has a strong natural tendency to pace, then you'll train him to the amble. From there it may be

The amble. Amblers naturally move in a more head-up, hollow frame. If this were a true square gait, the lifted fore leg would be more vertical to the ground. Here it's ready to be set down immediately after the same-side lateral hind.

possible to bring out a nice running walk. You'll seldom get such a laterally gaited horse more diagonally gaited than this.

As with the other gaits, ask the horse for more speed. When you sense the horse breaking into a pace, shift your weight from one stirrup to another while using your rein to swing the horse's head from side to side. You'll have to experiment to figure out the best timing and action for this. If necessary, stand up in your stirrups to get a stronger weight shift.

Training for the Rack

I hesitate to even use the term 'rack' because it's become so associated with the high-stepping, Saddlebred show gait. Many people would

Swinging the horse's head from side to side using a leading rein while shifting your weight from one stirrup to the other should help break up the two-beat gait of a flat pace. (It also helps to cure the trot.)

125

Above, Laura Fredericks rides Merry Boy's Spirit F-88 at a true rack. His stride is short and–if you could see it in motion–there is only moderate head shaking. There is strong contact on the bit, because she's asking him to quicken and shorten stride. Usually at some point in this gait there is only one foot on the ground.

call the gait I'm describing here an amble. But for our purposes–and the sake of consistency–I prefer to call the intermediate, square single-footing gait a rack, and the more lateral stepping pace an amble. Some folks will no doubt disagree, as there has never been any widely accepted distinctions established for these two intermediate gaits. Often the catchall term 'single-footing' is used for both. Yet they are distinctly different.

Most gaited horses are capable of performing the rack–some fox trotters being the most common exception. This gait is is a walk performed with animation at speed, with little or no over-stride and only slight to moderate head nod. It is usually easy to bring out in any horse with the capacity to gait.

Here Laura has asked Spirit for a running walk. His body frame and stride have lengthened. There is more relaxed contact with the bit, allowing Spirit to stretch out his topline to produce more head nod. There are always two or three feet on the ground.

To encourage the rack, ask the horse for more speed, keep it on a fairly short rein (but don't overflex the horse's neck) and refuse to allow it to break into a trot or pace. If it trots, paces, fox trots or ambles, bring it back down and start over. You'll know you've got it right when the gait feels fast, smooth and flowing, the timing of the footfalls is evenly spaced, and the horse exhibits moderate head nod.

The Running Walk

The running walk can take some time to develop, but is well worth the effort. Plan to do many, many miles of riding at a flat energetic walk. When the horse is moving in a quick, loose manner at the walk, ask for a lengthened stride and bit more speed. But just a bit. You want him to keep the true walk's strong head-nodding, deep understriding form. If the horse begins to shorten stride, lifts his head and quickens his gait, then you've got a fox trot or rack rather than a true running walk. Bring him back down to a flat walk, let him loosen up, and try again. Use your legs and seat to encourage his hind leg to reach farther underneath himself with every stride. Ask for greater speed through lengthened stride. Keep a moderate–not tight nor loose–hold on the reins, and allow your hands to follow the motion of his head with each stride. When he gets really loose and walking, this will involve some motion in your shoulders and arms as well, though you should avoid 'pumping' the reins. This may get him to shake his head, but will do nothing to encourage the true, deep head nod of the running walk.

It's a simple fact of life that not all horses *can* perform the running walk. The hallmark of one who can is the horse's ability to use his hind legs to overstep the track of his front foot by at least several inches. Some horses overtrack by as much as two feet. At the same time there is a rolling, reaching, loose action in the shoulder that enables his front end to keep pace with his hindquarters. Many people think this gait is performed with a lot of action and quick strides, but this isn't necessarily–or preferably–true. When you're riding a good running walk, it often feels like you're in a simple, smooth walk. The only indication you have of any great speed is that you're leaving other non-gaited horses in the dust–or forcing their riders to endure a lot of trotting! This is because the secret to the Walking Horse's gait lies in it's depth and reach of stride, rather than it's quickness.

As the horse becomes established in this gait, it will become looser and more rhythmic. You'll discern a distinct and even 1–2–3–4 footfall sound, and the horse will move with increasingly deeper head nod.

Photo by Mickey Anderson

One simple way to teach your horse to canter is to ride behind a friend on an uphill incline. Gather your horse, place one foot slightly behind the girth, and use it to push the horse forward at the same time you push with your seat and give him more of his head. At the same time, have the rider in front of you cue their horse to canter. At first don't be too concerned with speed and collection—those things can come later. Initially you want to teach the horse to respond to your riding aids for a canter. Increasing collection and control will come later.

The Canter

The canter and the lope are essentially the same gait, except the lope is performed with a lower-slung frame and slightly less collection. English people 'canter,' while Western riders 'lope.' For our purposes here, I'll use the term canter.

Training the horse to canter under saddle is usually not a difficult proposition. I start them at the bottom of a moderate incline. As the horse heads up the hill, I ask for slightly increased collection. Once I've obtained this, I lean slightly forward in the saddle, move one leg behind the girth, and give him a good boot while 'releasing' his collected energy through the rein. Most of the time the horse will immediately spring forward into a nice, easy canter. This is doubly true if you're riding with another horse, and they take up the canter just before you ask your horse for it. This often causes the horse to spring into a canter before he's even had time to think about it, or get confused by the new signals you're sending. Horses do not like getting left behind by their friends! By the time he realizes what's happened, you've repeated the exercise often enough that he's responding to the aids automatically.

On occasion–usually with a horse that tends toward pacing–you'll get a horse that wants to cross canter. This means to take up the canter with different leads fore and hind. You'll know this has happened if it suddenly feels like you're being vigorously bounced out of the saddle at every stride. Bring the horse back down to a walk *immediately.* Cross cantering is dangerous, as there is the very real possibility of the horse kicking a fore foot with a hind foot, and literally knocking himself over. Not good. *Very* not good. Chapter six offers suggestions for working with a horse with this tendency.

Once your horse will canter on an incline, ask him to do so while working him in the arena, using the same aids you used on the hill. Always ask for a canter transition from the walk. Never try to rush or hurry your horse into a canter from a trot or other faster gait, as this will encourage him to move in an unbalanced, front-heavy frame. After he's learned the basic canter, your goal is to teach him to move on the correct lead and in a balanced, non-hurried fashion. This is easiest accomplished by working in a circle in an enclosed area. Make certain the horse's muscles are warmed up and he's in a relaxed frame of mind. Do a few bends and circles at the walk. Ask for some collection, and then send him forward with your leg behind the girth. For a circle to the right, I push the horse forward with my left (outside) foot while lifting the right (inside) rein *ever so slightly.* This is reversed for a circle to the left. Different trainers use different methods and cues–I'm only telling you what works best for me.

Once the horse is cantering in a smooth, rhythmic manner and at a controlled speed, you may ask for more or less speed by shortening and lengthening stride with more, or less, collection.

Lead Changes

To teach a horse to change leads, work him in a canter on a large figure 8 pattern. When you get to the center of the pattern, bring him back down to a walk and cue him to canter on the changed lead. This may initially take several strides. Shorten the number of transition strides as he gets comfortable with this–don't be in too big of a rush–until you can ask for a switch with only one walk stride in between lead changes. From here it's a simple matter to ask for a flying lead change, with no downward gait transition. Gather the horse just before you intend to ask for a change, and give him the usual cues for a canter, on the lead opposite to the one on which he's been traveling. In only a couple of days you'll both have this down so pat that you'll be tempted to try some pole bending exercises. (And why not?)

Allow your horse to take a few transition steps in the center of the figure eight before asking for a lead change. Lessen the number of steps until he can switch leads without changing gait.

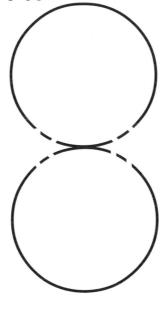

Chapter Six
Dealing with Gait Problems

I suspect this is the section that motivated most of my readers to purchase this book. I wish there could have been a faster way to get to this subject. In fact I was tempted to put this chapter toward the front of the book. But to do so would have shortchanged my readers in the long run because in all honesty, there are no quick solutions nor 'magic buttons' that will help get a horse to perform his saddle gait. While the solution to our gait problems are often straightforward and uncomplicated, it is still going to take time and persistence to work things out. There are no substitutes for good basic horsemanship, as outlined in the previous chapters. I highly recommend that you study the previous chapter before attempting to deal with gait problems. Often good foundational elementary training and conditioning techniques are all that's needed.

Nevertheless, if you own or have purchased a gaited horse, and need some help *right now*, there are a few things I can suggest. Try each approach to the problem for a long enough period of time that you know it won't work before going on to the next attempt. Otherwise you risk getting the horse more mixed up than he already is, and exacerbating rather than solving the difficulty.

Is there *Really* a Problem?

The first thing you need to determine is whether or not there is really a problem with the horse. Too often the real trouble is that we maintain unreasonable expectations of our horses. Only you can decide if this is the case in your situation.

First, ask yourself if the horse is performing a comfortable saddle gait–regardless of what that gait might be. If so, what is your reason for wanting to make changes? Is he tripping or stumbling, making him unsafe to ride? Do you need to get him to perform a different intermediate gait for the show ring? For example, is your Tennessee Walking Horse fox trotting, and you want him to be able to compete in Walking Horse show classes? Or is your Missouri Fox Trotter too racky for the show ring? These are problems that can usually be solved.

On the other hand, if you use your horse strictly for personal pleasure, and your only reason for wanting to change his gait is so that he'll be performing as such a horse (presumably) *should*, then perhaps you should reconsider. Why fix something that's not really broken? Chances are, your horse is performing the gait that is easiest and most comfortable for him. If it's comfortable for you as well, then what's the problem? This is especially true if you ride the horse infrequently–twice a week or less. To try to get him to change his way of going without being willing to devote the time and effort required to build up the necessary muscles and flexibility will be counterproductive. It will only create new, more complex problems for you and the horse.

You may simply enjoy the challenge of making your horse the best he can be, as opposed to trying to simply 'fix' him to do something different than what he's doing. Overall improvement is a valid and worthwhile goal. If this is what you want, however, you should know that the best way to get long-lasting benefits is by practicing the exercises and riding techniques explained in chapter five. You can accomplish a great deal–and help keep a positive attitude in your horse–by adapting the exercises to the trail. This doesn't change the fact that you must be willing to really *ride* your horse every minute you're mounted, as opposed to simply relaxing and going along on him as a relatively passive passenger. Improvement will take place over months, as opposed to days or weeks. But if you enjoy the challenge of enhancing your own, as well as your horse's, athletic abilities–and riding a truly athletic, light and responsive horse–then there's no better route to take.

The Casual Rider

For many horse lovers this kind of structured, attentive riding is sheer boredom. Their idea of having a good time is simply to relax and enjoy the scenery and the companionship of other riders. There's nothing wrong with this! We own horses for our own pleasure. If we begin to allow other folks' standards to dictate our own, then we miss out on a lot. As casual riders, the two factors that we must consider outside of our own desires are safety–ours and others'–and the overall well-being of the horse. Those considerations mandate that we become knowledgeable enough, and remain sufficiently active in the saddle, to keep the horse obedient to basic riding aids. Anything less of a commitment to good basic horsemanship skills is short-sighted and irresponsible.

In order to be safe, and have a genuinely pleasurable riding experience, we need to have a horse who is well trained to neck rein. He needs to be more attentive to the rider than to the other horses, to go when we say go, and stop when we say stop. He must be mannerly around other horses, and relatively sure-footed even over rough terrain. In addition, a horse that will be primarily used on the trail should be able to be mounted from either side, and be able to perform a simple rein back. While many riders never use their legs or seat as riding aids, it's advisable to teach the horse to at least move off your leg pressure. This simple maneuver can get you, and others around you, out of some dangerous spots! Commit yourself to this level of riding, and you'll owe apologies to no one.

If you really enjoy being on a horse, but don't appreciate the challenges of training or working with them, then your best bet is to be doubly certain that the animal you purchase is exactly what you want, and will perform a good saddle gait as naturally as other horses trot. It's also a good idea to buy an older, well-seasoned mount–I recommend one who is seven years or older. Most horses still have some tom-foolery left in them until this age.

Common Gait Problems

The most common complaint among gaited horse owners is that their horse refuses to do anything under saddle but a flat trot or pace. Either problem can be extremely frustrating to the person who bought a horse with the assumption they were going to be riding a smooth, comfortably gaited horse. Whether we're trying to get a fox trot, a rack, or a running walk, the cure for these problems is essentially the same. In any of these cases, the trotting horse needs to become more laterally gaited, and the pacing horse needs to become more diagonally inclined. The horses need to be 'squared up.'

No Trotting Allowed

The first and easiest tactic to try with a horse that wants to trot is simply not to allow him to do so. Every time he starts to break into a trot, bring him back to a walk. Continue to ask for extended stride and more speed–not too much at any one time. Ride him to and then at the point where he wants to break gait, but don't allow him to do so under any circumstances. What should happen is that he will be able to go faster and faster without breaking to the trot. This can be especially effective through heavy mud, deep grass and on downhill inclines, since these situations all tend to break up the two-beat synchrony between the front and hind diagonals.

You may suddenly feel a that your horse has changed gaits, but is not doing a hard trot. Your seat feels a different, shuffling action in the hind, and the head is definitely bobbing more up and down than at the walk. Chances are he's picked up a fox trot, which is halfway between a walk and a trot. If you like the fox trot–and most people definitely *do*–then you're home free. Just keep on doing what you're doing for as long and as often as possible.

If, however, you're determined to teach your horse to perform a rack or true running walk, then don't allow him to fox trot either. Simply bring him back to a walk, and ride him for hours and hours and miles and miles this way. Once he's well muscled and had lots of warming up, begin to ask for slightly increasing speed and greater length of stride. (Techniques for this are explained in chapter five.) When you feel his hind leg moving forward, use a strong pushing, sliding seatbone to *push* the horse into a longer stride, side to side. You should actually be able to feel the horse lengthen his stride in response to your cue. This can be a lot of work for the rider, short term, but will pay big dividends over time.

Curing the Trot

You may acquire a horse who's already learned to trot. A horse that refuses to perform anything but a hard trot in spite of our best efforts on the trail needs to learn how to break up his gait so that it's at least slightly more lateral. There are a number of things we can do to encourage this. But we need to realize that unless the horse has an inherent ability to perform a lateral gait, he will *never* be able to do so, regardless of your techniques and efforts.

Are you sure that both—or at least one—of the horses' parents were genuinely gaited? Does he have a sufficiently sloping pelvis to indicate an ability to gait? Have you seen the horse gaiting freely in the pasture, or while under another rider? Will he gait on the longe line? If the answer to these questions is 'no,' then it won't hurt to still work at getting a natural gait out of the horse. But be willing to accept the possibility that your horse may never be able to perform a smooth saddle gait. Most horses that possess the inherent ability to gait will exhibit it naturally at some time or another. Our first order of business is get the horse working in a round, supple frame. He needs to be able to bend his body from side to side, and to softly stretch the muscles of his topline, all along the croup and back and up the entire length of his neck. This ability to flex and stretch is the secret to obtaining long-strided, well-balanced gait.

Photo by Mickey Anderson

This horse's lovely way of going disproves the contention that long-shanked walking horse bits are always 'cruel.' He's nicely up on the bit, soft and giving to his rider's (evidently sensitive) hands and seat. A close-up of his head shows a soft eye with no sign of pain or discomfort.

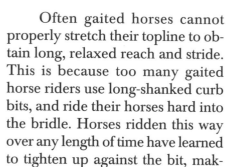

Often gaited horses cannot properly stretch their topline to obtain long, relaxed reach and stride. This is because too many gaited horse riders use long-shanked curb bits, and ride their horses hard into the bridle. Horses ridden this way over any length of time have learned to tighten up against the bit, making their entire bodies hard. We need to teach them that it won't hurt to soften up.

I have nothing against such curbs *per se*–indeed, the right bit used with sensitive hands and seat can help a horse to round out and perform his gait. But it's never a good idea to push the horse too hard into the bridle, regardless of the gait. To do so will cause the horse to stiffen the muscles along his back, neck and poll, and shorten his strides. This in turn will prevent him from being able to round out his body to get strong under-reach behind and long stride length with his front limbs. The end result is a stiff, uncomfortable way of going–for the horse, if not for the rider. Such riding is guaranteed to cause physical problems for the horse over the long-term, and prevent him from moving in a soft, round and supple way during the short term.

If you're not seeing/feeling the horse stretch his top muscles forward with each stride, you need to help him do this. Start by putting him in a milder bit, if possible. I say 'if possible' because some gaited horses who have been trained and ridden in long-shanked curb bits all their lives will absolutely not respond to a milder bit, be it snaffle or curb. They have learned to depend on the action of the bit to 'hold them up,' and when you try to switch to something milder, they lean into it so hard that they nearly fall down. Such horses are known as 'borers.'

I would have been the first person, a couple of years ago, to argue that any horse can be taught to work well off a snaffle bit, though I'd heard otherwise a time or two. Then I met the horse who changed my mind. (There's always one of those out there, lurking around in the bushes, or at the local auction house!) Though well-gaited, this gelding was stiff in the neck and more than a little strong willed. I figured the best way to handle the problem was to put him in a mild snaffle bit and work on circle and bending exercises, to get him to soften and loosen up, and make him more responsive to my aids. By the way, this is usually the best approach when dealing with *any* kind of horse problem.

I was about to embark on a learning experience. When I tried to ride him in this bit, he leaned so hard into the bridle that it nearly pulled my arms out of their sockets. I figured this problem could be handled in short order. I put him on the longe line and did various ground exercises with him for awhile in the snaffle bit, encouraging him to relax and give to it. Then we went back to mounted work again, but to no avail. The longer I worked at this, the worse he behaved–and there was nothing I could do about it. The more helpless I became, the more he took advantage. When I realized he wasn't ever going to adapt to the snaffle mouthpiece, I tried a mild, short-shanked curb bit–again without success. By now he was becoming downright rebellious every time I mounted up. The *only* bit he would agree to work in was the walking horse bit to which he was accustomed. I finally wised up, and we worked with that bit!

My suggestion is to work your horse in the mildest bit that he will accept. Try a thick O or D-ring snaffle bit first. It may have either a rubber, sweet iron or stainless steel mouthpiece. Simple snaffle bits (in my opinion) aren't the best bit to use to produce good long-striding gaits. They *are* good to work with when you need to teach your horse to stretch and bend and give to the bit.

If your horse refuses to work in such a bit, try a thick mullen-mouth bit with sliding cheeks, so you've got something that will work on his bars and the corners of his mouth, but won't give him a port or joint in his mouth to resist. It's been my observation that many gaited horses work especially well in this kind of bit.

If absolutely necessary, you may go back to his regular long-shanked curb bit, but clip your reins on to the space right at the mouth, rather than at the shank ends. This will give you a more direct contact with his mouth and limit the action of the curb, while helping him to feel he's working in something safe and familiar. The bottom line is, when we're having problems with our horses, we have to do whatever humane thing will work–which will vary from horse to horse.

No matter what kind of bit you use, there is no substitute for soft, giving hands–which comes out of a sensitive, well-balanced seat. You've got to be *with* your horse's every move. This is more important than the type of bit you choose to use. If you've never had riding lessons and/or professional evaluation of your skills, you might consider doing so. Nothing but a good rider will ever produce a good horse, gaited or otherwise. If you're not inter-ested in improving your riding skills, then you'll need an older, well-trained and gaited horse to start.

Once you've got your horse properly bitted, take him through Exercises 1, 2, 4 and 5 from chapter five. It may take two or three weeks to get the horse loose, bending and supple and stretching his topline the way you want, but it will be time well-spent.

When the horse is moving in a soft and supple manner under saddle, begin to do lateral work with him. Ask for more and more

Simple O-Ring Snaffle Bit

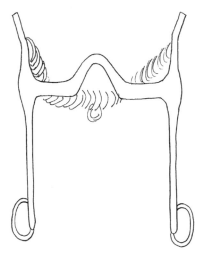

Curb Bit

Mullen Mouth Bit

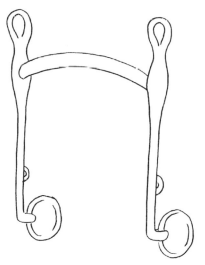

speed at this work. Chances are, he'll want to trot when he reaches a certain speed. When this happens, use your aids to 'bump' his haunches over into two-track, first one direction, and then the other. Keep a well-balanced seat, avoid leaning forward, sit deep in the saddle and use your seat bones to reinforce your leg aids. It's likely that at some point this work is going to break up the trot, taking the diagonal pairs of legs out of synchrony with one another. Now you've got the fox trot, or the rack.

When you feel this happen, praise the horse, and keep riding him at this gait for as long as he will maintain it. At first this may only be for a few steps. If you feel the gait becoming hard again–more jarring and up-and-down motion–ask for more two-tracking until he's back into gait. Your goal is to get him to recognize that you *want* him to work in the gait, and get him used to doing it. You're not only working with his mental understanding, but helping to build 'muscle memory,' so that the more lateral gait becomes a natural response, both mentally and physically, when you ask for an upward gait transition.

Another Method

If your horse still hasn't broken up the hard trot, you might try 'swinging' him from one side to another using your rein and body weight. This can be especially effective on a downhill slope. Take the horse to the top of a hill–as steep as you feel comfortable riding. If your horse tends to stumble, don't make it *too* steep, or you could be asking for big trouble. On the way down, ask for more speed. When the horse is trotting, stand in your stirrups and pull his head from side to side using a direct pull on each rein, while shifting your weight from one stirrup to another. Make both the weight shift and the swinging action as exaggerated and strong as possible. By the time you reach the bottom of the hill, the horse should be fox trotting or racking. Use every downhill incline you come to as a practice arena until the horse can 'break it up' on either the flat or downhill.

By the way, this is one time when a heavier rider can come in handy. A heavy rider increases a horse's tendency toward lateral gait, especially on the downhill. If you're a real light weight, work in a very heavy western saddle, and securely strap on a saddle bag filled with a few college textbooks. (You always knew they'd come in handy for teaching *something*, didn't you?)Do whatever you have to do to put a heavier weight on the horse's back.

Another technique that sometimes works is to ride the horse with another gaited horse. I've found that it's very common for one horse to pick up the footfall pattern and rhythm of a companion animal without even thinking about it. In fact I own a non-gaited Appaloosa mare who has been known to perform a passable rack when on the trail in the company of my Walking Horse gelding!

Ride for long enough to loosen your horse up, and then ask your helper to put his or her horse into gait at a speed just a bit faster than what your horse likes to break gait at–and do not allow your horse to do so. You'll need a riding companion who's sensitive to what you're trying to do, and who won't mind slowing down to keep you from getting so far behind that your horse begins to rush, and pay you little attention. The goal is to get everybody to relax and move out without getting nervous and uptight. If you do this, these 'riding exercises' can turn into a real delight.

Curing the Pace

Pacing is by far the most common complaint among gaited horse owners. I believe it may be easier to work with than trotting–though many people would certainly disagree. The reason I believe this is because so many horses who trot have absolutely *no* inherited ability to make their gait more lateral. On the other hand, most pacing horses have some trotting blood somewhere in their background. If so, they can almost always be conditioned and taught to square up, to one degree or another. Some will never square out to anything more than an amble–but others can be trained to perform a wonderful running walk. The secret to working with a pacey horse is–again–conditioning, conditioning, and more conditioning.

Many pacey horses tend to have long, hollow backs, long weak hindquarter coupling, long hind legs with high set hocks, 'waspy' waists and 'slab sides.' This conformation makes it difficult for them to coil their loins and to bend their frame laterally. Their natural inclination is to move in an uncollected, 'strung out' body frame. Pacing is simply easier for them because of their inherent physical limitations.

We need to help them overcome those limitations, and make it easier to collect, coil at the loins, and bend laterally. While we can't change the horse's basic body structure, we can certainly improve its overall strength, agility and condition.

The first gaited horse I ever bought was your typical pacey horse. She was out of a long line of Big Lick show horses. I figured this meant she must have inherited great gaiting ability! Little did I know that she, like most Big Lick horses, could pace while standing still. When I purchased her, she had been stall-bound for several years and was totally out of condition. (In fact, pity was one deciding factor of the purchase–ignorance a close second!) While she had some shortcomings, she also had many fine qualities. I didn't anticipate that one of the greatest benefits I would receive from her was an education–she gave me strong incentive, right off the bat, to get reliable information about how to deal with an *extremely* pacey horse.

When we brought this mare home, the only thing she knew to do was walk and pace. To her credit, she possessed the fastest, smoothest flat walk of any horse I've ever ridden, before or since. That's probably what kept her in our barn and out of the sale ring! At nine years of age, she'd never been taught to respond to leg aids, except to speed up which, in her case, meant pacing at breakneck speed. She'd been ridden in nothing other than a saddleseat saddle, and did not neck rein at all. My husband (whose horse she was purported to be) rode nothing but western. She had also never–and I do mean *never*–been out of sight of other horses. I'll let you imagine how much fun we had together for the first several weeks.

The reason I share all this is because I want you to be assured that if *this* horse could learn to collect, take up an intermediate gait, and become attentive and obedient to all the riding aids, then so could almost any horse you might ever come across. She did all this, and more–as will your problem pacer.

Useful Exercises

The first line of business with pacey horses is to teach them to stretch, bend, engage their loins, and collect their entire frame. The best way to accomplish this is by practicing the full range of exercises in chapter five. Emphasize bending, lateral movements, neck stretching, and varying stride length exercises especially. Teach the horse to collect. This work needs to be accomplished at a slow speed, especially to start. It may take several weeks to get your horse soft, strong and supple enough to be able to break up the pace even a little bit. If you know this going in, then you should be better able to relax and enjoy the process, which will help both you and your horse.

Vary your exercise routine with cross country riding at the walk and flat walk. This will help your horse to keep a sweet attitude, and build the body strength that is required for an intermediate gait. Also, when you do cavalletti work, set the poles 3"-4" up off the ground and ask for increased speed after your horse has become accustomed to working over them at ground level. This work strongly encourages the trot, and makes the pace impos-

Uphill work encourages the horse to work off it's haunches and take deep strides. It's also great for both aerobic and muscular conditioning.

Photo by Mickey Anderson

sible. Your horse may pace between poles, and trot over them. That's OK for starters. She's getting the idea, and building those all-important muscles for a more diagonal gait.

At no time during this training period should you ride your horse to the point of exhaustion. This will encourage her to fall back into a sagging, strung-out frame, and be totally counterproductive to your goals. Limit the exercises to fifteen or twenty minutes to start, and increase your riding time to an hour or so over a month's time. You'll need to judge your horse's capabilities yourself, so keep an alert eye for signs of fatigue.

And Here's. . .the Gait!

When your horse is well-conditioned and working well in a modest curb bit, then it's time to focus on getting a good intermediate gait. Take her outside and ride her at a brisk flat walk until she's loosened up and relaxed. Then ask her to collect and lengthen her stride. Lengthen the amount of time she is ridden like this until she will move along comfortably at a rack or running walk for as long as you want. As with breaking up the trot, it might be

146

of some benefit to ride her alongside another gaited horse and see if she will more naturally pick up the speed and rhythm of the gait that way.

If she still tends to be too pacey, ride her up hills as fast as she will go at the walk. Sit deep and push with both legs. This encourages the horse to round her topline and work strongly off the haunches, and to take long reaching strides with the back legs. It's entirely likely that your horse will perform a true running walk when traveling up hills. Use this to your advantage by asking for more speed and collection going uphill, and moving at a slow walk going down. (Downhill work encourages the pace.)

Besides uphill work, riding your horse at ever-increasing speed through deep grass or rough-going ground–such as sand, snow or newly plowed fields–will very likely break up the pace and help produce a nice rack or running walk. Remember that this is very hard work, and bring the horse along gradually.

Another tip: while heavy riders can help eliminate the trot, the opposite is true of pacey horses. Don't expect the horse to gait under a large rider until the conditioning and training process is in its final stages. These horses, being often very large and well-boned, appear to be able to handle large riders easily. But looks are deceiving, since a long back and weak hindquarter coupling lessens weight-bearing abilities. For the sake of keeping the horse's back from tightening up, if you're a heavy rider–weighing more than 20% of the horse's body weight, or 200 pounds for a 1,000 pound horse–then dismount every hour or so and walk alongside for ten minutes. This will allow the horse to rest and stretch its back muscles when you're on long rides.

Still Not Gaiting?

If your horse still isn't gaiting well after you've consistently tried all of these techniques, then you'll probably have to concede that he's doesn't possess a natural ability to gait. The only other thing you can reasonably change is the way that the horse is trimmed and shod, or saddled. Before giving up entirely, check out chapter seven on those subjects. If possible, find a farrier experienced with gaited horses to work with you. Perhaps a little longer foot, change of angle, or slightly heavier shoe, will allow you to obtain the gait you want. Or maybe you really need a better fitting saddle.

Your other alternatives are to simply learn to enjoy the trot– or buy a horse with the proven ability to gait under saddle.

Canter Problems

Most canter problems are experienced with pacey horses. It's simply too hard for them to coil their loins and move their legs in a diagonally-oriented fashion. The same routines that work for curing the pace will work for improving the canter. Most useful is uphill riding–in fact, if you did little else, I would suggest that you ask the horse for a canter at every uphill incline. If he tends to cross-canter (as many pacey horses do), bring him back down to a walk and ask for greater collection before you push him into the canter. Exaggerate your riding aids, giving a very strong push with your seat and outside leg, while lifting the inside rein a bit more than usual. Work on cantering in tighter and tighter circles. Use a light weight rider for this work until the horse is well conditioned and 'set' for performing the canter. Never–and I mean never–canter the animal downhill.

Don't insist that the horse canter like a non-gaited horse. The action may be more lateral in both sequence and rhythm. Be content if the gait is performed on the correct and matching leads, and in a balanced fashion. My favorite horse has a very lateral canter that's smooth as silk.

Running Walk or Rack to Fox Trot

It may be that your fox trotting horse prefers to do a rack or running walk. The best cure for this is fast cavalletti work, which encourages a more diagonal gait. It also helps to pick the horse's head up a bit more–don't overdo this–and ask for frequent half-halts to get him to move his weight farther back over his haunches. You'll need to work with someone on the ground who knows how to distinguish the gaits so you'll recognize when the horse gets it right, and be praising and practicing at the correct times. When riding cross country, uphill work will encourage more diagonal action. A change in bitting may also be in order. You'll need to experiment with this to see what works best. Ask your farrier for help also (see chapter seven).

Fox Trot to Rack or Running Walk

You may want to produce a good rack or running walk gait from a horse that prefers to fox trot. Only a horse with the conformational ability for long overstride will be able to do a running walk–so be willing to content yourself with the rack, if need be.

Start by riding many, many miles at a brisk flat walk, loosening the horse up before asking for a modest increase in speed. As soon as the horse breaks to a fox trot, bring it back to the flat walk and start over. A horse's natural tendency when asked for too much speed, too soon, is to fall into a gait that is either more diagonal or lateral. Your goal is to get a perfect intermediate gait. There really are no shortcuts for this–the horse must relax, stretch and slightly drop his head, and reach deeply underneath with his hind legs. The spiral exercise from chapter five is an excellent one to try to obtain the results you want. Work the animal downhill often, as this will encourage more lateral motion. Use your seat and legs vigorously with each stride, pushing for more extension and rolling action. Get the horse to stretch his neck, and then softly round his poll and collect with true bit contact. Sometimes a bit with a deeper port and longer shanks can help. I recommend keeping a variety of bits on hand–you never know which one will bring out the best in a particular horse until you've tried it.

Check chapter seven for shoeing suggestions that may enable your diagonally inclined horse to square up.

Stumbling and Forging

A good, naturally gaited horse is usually very sure-footed, since there is always at least one foot–and usually two or three–on the ground at any given time. Unfortunately some of the traits that have become popular in the gaited horse show rings have detracted from this wonderful quality. If we own a horse that comes from a show horse background, then we may run into problems with stumbling. This seemingly innocent vice can be extremely dangerous. More than one person has been killed on a simple hack when the horse stumbled and fell, throwing its rider over its head and then falling on top of them.

Some lines of Missouri Fox Trotters have been bred for an exaggeratedly low-slung, long reach in front. This limits their ability to lift their front limbs very high from the ground. Such a horse can be a real challenge to ride across varied terrain as it wants to drag its toes in the dust. This is especially challenging when traveling uphill.

Tennessee Walking Horses sometimes demonstrate the opposite problem–an inability to lift their hind legs high enough to clear simple ground obstacles, leading to stumbling behind.

Much stumbling is caused by nothing more than laziness and inattentiveness, however. So the first tact to try if you ride a stumbler is to take a sharp snatch on the reins every time the horse misses a step, quickly press both legs into his sides, and tell him to "Pick them up!" It's always a good idea to be a very active rider on such an animal, to keep them alert to what's going on. They tend to tune out, or daydream, while going down the trail. Such a horse with a tuned-out, daydreaming rider can be a dangerous combination!

Regardless of the reason for stumbling–conformational or temperamental–to encourage the horse to learn to pick up its feet, do some cavalletti exercises. Riding over varied terrain and crossing natural obstacles also help. Usually just a few weeks of good riding will cure the stumbler. Allowing them plenty of natural turnout in the pasture also teaches them to watch out for themselves.

Some horses with clogged tear ducts have been known to be stumblers. Your vet can determine if this is a problem, and perform a simple routine to unclog these ducts, if necessary.

Forging–or hitting a front limb with a hind limb while being ridden–is another potentially dangerous problem, and not uncommon with our gaited stock. It can cause the horse to unexpectedly knock its front legs out from under itself, making it fall dangerously forward. At times the hind foot may step on the heel of the front shoe, pulling it right off–with perhaps a big chunk of foot with it. Horses with an especially long under reach are particularly at risk. Forging is often at least partly due to inattention and laziness on the part of the horse. Encourage him to move forward in a balanced, collected manner, and you'll soon find that his front legs move out of the way in plenty of time to avoid being struck by the hind legs.

You might also need to enlist your farrier's help to eliminate stumbling or forging. Helpful suggestions along these lines are included in chapter seven.

Saddle Considerations

A poorly fitting or designed saddle may cause faulty gait, stumbling, unwillingness to go downhill, uphill, move forward or bend. The trouble may be rooted in any one of several possibilities: a too-narrow or too-wide tree, a pommel that rests directly on the horse's withers, or one that is placed right on top of the shoulder blade, restricting motion and causing pain with every stride. Occasionally the saddle is too long for a short-backed horse. This makes it difficult for the animal to bend as the rear edge of the saddle pokes sharply into his hip while the front edge hits the shoulder blade. The problem may be that the saddle is too small for the rider, providing poor weight distribution and placing too much pressure on one area of the horse's back. A poorly designed or constructed saddle may also cause this problem, or else cause the rider's weight to rest too far forward or back of the horse's center of gravity. If any one of these situations exist, it will detract from your horse's comfort, and abilities. Oftentimes a horse is suffering from more than one of these problems. Since we humans are so prone to error, we must never be too quick to charge anything against the horse.

If you're experiencing problems with your horse, check immediately to make sure that the saddle you're using is well-designed, and appropriately fitted to both you and the horse. Chapter seven will help show you what to look for–and what to look out for–when fitting a saddle.

Chapter Seven
Bit, Saddle and Shoe

Fitting a horse to ride is one of those aspects of horseman-ship that is either made to seem extremely difficult and complex, or else is oversimplified and neglected. We should take a realistic approach. One doesn't need to be a physicist to figure out what works–but a basic knowledge of equine physiology doesn't hurt!

Saddle Fitting

As touched upon in the last chapter, poor-fitting saddles are the root cause of many of our riding difficulties. It's easy to un-derstand why. Imagine heading out for a 10-mile cross-country trek with a 30 or 40-pound child in a backpack. If the backpack is well-balanced across your hips, shoulders and buttocks, and the straps and fittings appropriately placed and adjusted–and you're conditioned for the walk–chances are you'll complete your jour-ney a bit weary, but happy.

Now imagine what that same trip would be like if the back-pack is so small and poorly designed that the child wiggles and turns all day in a vain effort to get comfortable. Furthermore, two aluminum braces poke into the center of your shoulder blades, so that every time you swing an arm, or the child wiggles, a brace digs deeply into your flesh right over the bone. Instead of the bottom of the pack resting across the top of your buttocks, the weight is carried over your shoulders on too-thin straps, and on the spot where the aluminum braces are cutting into you. Within a mile, your neck and shoulders are aching, your lower back hurts, and your shoulder blades are literally on fire. Each time the child moves–which remember, is nearly continually–your misery worsens. The only thing worse than having to go down a steep incline is having to drag yourself and your burden up one. Every step feels like it must be your last–but you've no recourse but to keep going.

Long before the end of this walk, your body will be stiffened in many places against the pain–which will cause you to move in an awkward, stiff manner. Your attitude will be sour. You'll be irritated with the child on your back, and letting him know it every time he does something to increase your discomfort. You'll probably be stumbling and tripping on things that would normally not affect you in the least. You'll want to rest often, will try to find ways to avoid hills, and certainly won't feel like going from a walk to a jog just because the child on your back starts jumping around and yelling at you to "Go faster!" At about that point the only thing preventing you from unceremoniously dumping your child in the woods is your inherent patience and love. (And a healthy respect for the law!)

So it is for our horses when we strap a poorly fitted saddle onto them. We should take care to make certain it is fitted correctly. This is far more important that what kind of saddle you decide to purchase and ride. Various types of saddles come into vogue at different times–for a couple of years everyone has to have an Australian stock saddle, then suddenly they're all raving about Plantation saddles. One group wouldn't be caught dead in anything but a Western style saddle–which of course, the hunt seat crowd views disdainfully. The truth is, any of these saddles can be appropriate for general riding purposes, so long as it correctly fits the horse and rider.

*English, Western, Australian, Plantation. . .leather, synthetic. . .racing, endurance, trail, show, pleasure. . .There is a saddle to fit every need, size, personality and life style. A prime consideration when considering the purchase of **any** type of saddle is that it be well-fitted to both horse and rider.*

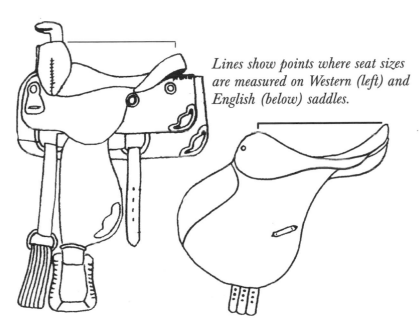

Lines show points where seat sizes are measured on Western (left) and English (below) saddles.

This photo shows how placing the rider's weight in a too-small saddle puts a great deal of pressure on a small area of the horse's back. Better to use a larger saddle for better weight distribution.

The seat size of a saddle is determined by the length of the seat from the back edge of the pommel back to the front edge of the cantle. If you're an average or small sized rider, look for a saddle with a small seat–14"-15" on a Western saddle; 16"-17" for an English style saddle. Otherwise you'll be sliding around on top of it all day, causing discomfort to your horse. You'll also be more securely seated in the event of an upset.

A large rider should look for a larger seated saddle–16" or 17" for a Western saddle, and 18" to 21" for an English style. Otherwise we're placing too much weight on too small an area of the horse's back, which will cause the animal to become sore and stiffen up. Many of today's saddle makers have finally conceded that Americans are getting bigger with each generation, and are making more saddles to fit our larger sizes. Until the last few years it was very difficult to find a 16" Western saddle. Now they're nearly as common as 15" seats–and 17" seats are becoming less rare as well. That's how it ought to be.

If you are a larger rider–as I am–you needn't be embarrassed about asking for and looking at only larger seat sizes. Though we may be in deep denial about our proportions, the truth is that other people size us up on sight. We're not really fooling anybody by looking at small or average sized saddles. Have you ever seen a large person squeezed into a small saddle? In a way, it makes us

appear foolish–rather like a fat lady shopping in a juniors depart-
ment store, or trying to squeeze into shoes two sizes too small. It
takes a mature person to simply acknowledge the facts, and purchase a saddle appropriate for his or her body type. Women especially tend to 'spread out' in the seat area as we mature–why be
ashamed to admit it? If this is the case with you, you're far from
alone. In real life there are more chubby grandma body types
than there are Cindi Crawfords!

Let's assume you sat on the saddle in the store, and found it
comfortable. Now it's time to try it on your horse. It's always wise
to try before you buy, or at least make certain you have liberal
return privileges. Initially, place the saddle on your horse over a
light sheet, rather than a thick saddle pad. You want to see how
well the saddle actually fits the horse. Saddle pads may cushion
the horse's back and help absorb sweat, but they should not be
expected to make up for a poorly fitted saddle. Going back to our
previous illustration, it might have helped you to have had a pad
placed between the backpacks and your back, but it wouldn't have
permanently solved the problem. Better to have a saddle that fits
correctly in the first place.

Make certain the saddle isn't placed on the horse directly
over the top of the scapula, or shoulder blade. Too often riders
position the saddle too far forward, causing it to cut into–and hinder
the motion of–the horse's shoulder. This can be a particular problem for our gaited horses, as they need to have a very loose-moving shoulder to perform a good intermediate gait. Many of them
also have a deeper, or more sloping, shoulder than non-gaited
horses, making it more likely to be a potential problem.

Use your fingers to feel exactly where the scapula is located,
then move the saddle back so that the edge rests at least three
inches behind this point. Any closer and it may hit the edge of the
scapula when the horse moves. Now look to see if this places the
rear of the saddle too close to the horse's hip, which will be restrictive when he tries to bend and turn. This is where our size can be
another consideration. I have a friend who owns a horse with a
remarkably short back. This is usually a desirable trait, as it in-

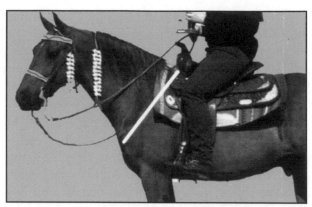

Oftentimes a horse cannot perform a good gait because the saddle has been positioned so that it hinders the movement of his shoulder when he steps forward. The white line on this photo shows the position of the shoulder. Imagine how this will be affected by the saddle when this MFT steps forward, and the top of the scapula rotates down and back.

creases the animal's weight-bearing capacity. The problem is, my friend no longer has a remarkably small derriere to match. Though she's owned the horse for several years, she has yet to find a saddle that is large enough to suit her, yet short enough to be entirely comfortable for her horse. To her credit, she keeps looking!

Having the rear of the saddle fall too far back on the horse might also place your own center of gravity behind the horse's, which will affect your riding balance and control. (The center of gravity is usually over and just behind the heart girth area, but shifts slightly forward at faster, collected saddle gaits, and even more forward at uncollected fast gaits). You won't be able to determine this for certain until you've actually ridden the saddle on the horse.

Now check to see how the saddle fits the contours of the horse's back. It should rest evenly all along the saddle's length, with no gaps or pressure points. If it's an English saddle, check to make certain the channel that runs through the middle of the underside stays in shape, rather than flattening out, when a rider sits in the saddle. Make sure the pommel doesn't rest too far down

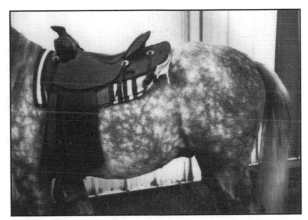

A comfortable, well-fitted saddle will give horse and rider many years of value.

over the horse's wither, especially when weight is placed in the saddle. There should be at least a two-inch clearance when the rider is in place. Is the tree wide enough? Check this at the fork, just under the pommel, to see that it sets comfortably over each side of the horse's wither, neither pinching nor leaving a gap. A too-narrow tree can be miserable for a horse, pinching the muscle on either side of the wither with every stride. One that's too wide will not distribute weight evenly, but will press into the horse on one point of each side of the wither. Ouch!

A good fit—and enough clearance—across the withers is important.

Many of these things I learned the hard way. For example, I once had a saddle that I absolutely loved to ride. When I placed it on a new horse, it seemed to fit just fine. When the horse developed a stilted, awkward way of going, I feared she was becoming navicular. It took me several weeks to figure out that the problem was with the saddle. It fit fine so long as it was placed directly on her back. But with a thick pad underneath, it became too narrow and pinched her upper shoulder and withers each time she took a step. I later discovered that the problem was nearly universal with that saddle on gaited horses–though it fit several non-gaited horses I'd ridden it on. That poor horse paid the price for my education and, let's hope, for some of yours!

Besides the basic saddle fit, carefully consider how it ought to be best rigged for your particular use. If you'll be traveling up hills, a well-fitted breast collar will help to prevent it from slipping too far backward. In our part of the country, cruppers are rare. They can help keep a saddle in place going downhill, especially if your horse has poor withers. If you decide to use a crupper, ask someone experienced in their use help you adjust it properly. I like to use a back cinch, adjusted so that there's light contact with the horse's underbelly. These are often buckled too loose, which may cause a horse that bucks or tries to kick at a fly to catch it's foot in the strap–*very* bad news. Also, if the horse jumps up or bucks, the loose strap will take hold *all at once,* which will further excite the horse and almost surely put you in greater peril. Pull a back cinch too tight, and you may find yourself on a bucking bronco! You want the rear cinch to keep the back end of the saddle from flying off your horse and slapping it hard in the kidneys if the horse gallops, falls or jumps around. Nothing more, nothing less.

How the saddle sits is largely a matter of personal preference. You should be able to keep your lower leg against the horse, and ride comfortably and balanced without leaning way forward or backward. We're all built so differently that I take exception to those who think there is only one right way to sit a saddle. What's right is what works best for you and your horse.

At right, Jamie had better hope Winston doesn't kick at a fly, or that loose back cinch could get them both into a world of trouble!

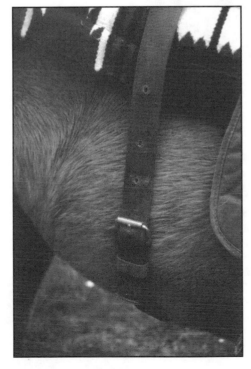

The rear cinch ought to be adjusted so that it is snug, but not tight. Check it over the course of the day, as they tend to loosen up.

If you ride a mare, then after she's had a foal or two her body shape will probably change. This might require refitting her for a new saddle. Often mares who 'lose' their gait after a foal or two are simply out of condition, and still being ridden in their ill-fitting 'maiden' saddles. As a rule, their withers become more prominent and their bodies grow wider. C'mon now, you ladies know how it is. . .!

Bitting

A curb bit is any bit with shanks, jointed or otherwise, and a snaffle bit is any bit with direct jointed action at the corners of the mouth, regardless of the mouthpiece. In common usage, horse people usually describe bits with jointed mouthpieces as snaffles, and bits with solid mouthpieces and shanks–with or without a port–as curb bits.

I've met people who insist their horses can perform a perfect intermediate gait in nothing more than a simple snaffle bit. To them, I truly lift my hat. Most people, myself included, believe they get better results with a well-balanced curb–yes, sometimes even those 'awful' long-shanked ones. I hear so many people decrying the use of these bits, as though there is never any good reason to use such a device. As a rule this is true–but there are exceptions to this rule, so don't be too quick to judge what other folks do.

I've seen people riding horses in so-called 'Tom Thumb' bits, thinking they're doing their horses a favor by using such a mild device. But those bits, with their jaw breaking 'nutcracker' effect between the jointed mouthpiece, jointed corners, curb strap and shanks, can be far harder on a horse's mouth and jaw than many so-called 'torture' bits. I also hear people complaining about the evils of 'gag' bits–yet in experienced hands these can be excellent training, or retraining, tools.

Truth is, the only harsh bit is the one in poor hands. If we're reasonably well-balanced, sensitive riders on well-trained horses, then there's no reason we can't employ a sophisticated bit. An appropriate curb bit in the right hands can help our horses to collect and set up in the proper body frame for gaiting. But please be aware that the longer the shanks, the more pronounced the port–and the tighter the curb chain–the greater potential there is for abuse of the bit. This doesn't mean we have to ride on a slack rein, only that we should never crank these bits to their maximum capacity. We want to teach our horses to trust us enough to softly come up *onto* the bit, rather than stiffen up against it or overbend to avoid it.

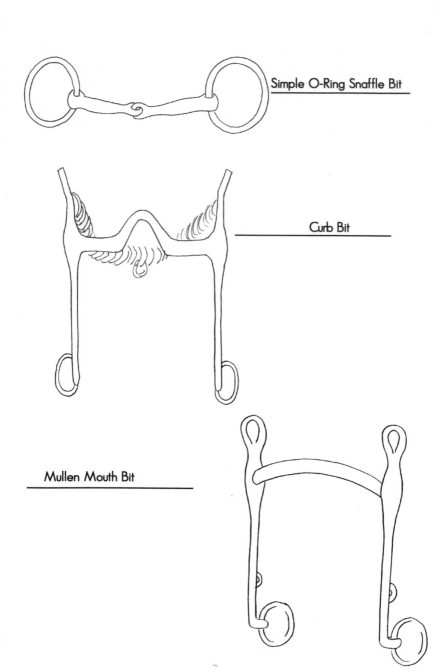

Simple O-Ring Snaffle Bit

Curb Bit

Mullen Mouth Bit

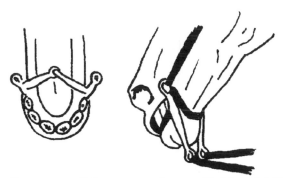

Above is an illustration of the actions of a so-called 'gentle' Tom Thumb bit. The jointed mouthpiece across the tongue and bars, combined with the jointed shanks and chin strap, can have a vicious 'nutcracker' effect on the hapless animal's mouth. This is actually a more severe bit than many regular shanked curbs. Since many people don't understand that, they're not as careful in their use of it—which can lead to the horse becoming stiff and resistant. This in turn will affect gait.

If you don't want to spend any time learning good riding skills–and that's OK–disregard what I said about using a sophisticated bit. Your best bet is to buy a very well-trained horse who will go along on a slack rein in a very mild curb or simple snaffle.

Always start a young horse in a simple snaffle–or, if you prefer and know how to use them, a bosal or hackamore. Teach the basics of collection in this equipment before introducing your horse to a curb bit of any kind. When you do go to a curb, start out with a mild one and only graduate to more complex devices as the horse learns how to properly round out and respond. In most cases, a low-port or mullen-mouth bit with a moderate (3"-5") shank is all that is required to encourage excellent gaiting action. Long 'walking horse' shanked bits are more a matter of tradition than necessity, and should be avoided. One exception to this may be a horse who has long been accustomed to being ridden in a demanding bit, and responds appropriately to it. If you feel you need such a bit to control your horse then it's time for some retraining. And not just for the horse.

To fit a bit, make sure that the mouthpiece is the right size to fit across your horse's mouth, being neither too narrow nor too wide. A 5"-wide mouthpiece is standard–but not all horses are standard sized. Some require a 5-1/2" wide mouthpiece, while others are better fitted with only a 4-1/2" one.

The bit should lay across the horse's tongue at the bars–the space that has no teeth. The mouthpiece must have enough of a curve, or a wide enough port, to leave plenty of room for the tongue. Make certain it's at least 3/4"-1" thick. Anything thinner will cut into the tongue and bars of the horse's mouth. If your horse is a male, check to be sure the wolf teeth don't hit against the bit, no matter what rein action you take. A bit that constantly hits against these teeth can cause the poor horse considerable pain, leading to head tossing and other unpleasant evasions. Wolf teeth serve no useful function and, like our wisdom teeth, are routinely extracted. This can be done by any equine veterinarian.

Speaking of dentistry, you'll want to be sure that your horse doesn't have any mouth sores as a result of jagged or misaligned

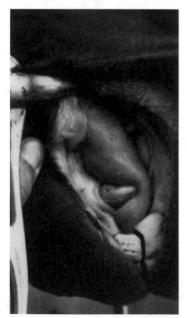

Geldings and stallions have 'wolf teeth' that occasionally interfere with the bit. This can cause the poor horse a great deal of distress. Such teeth serve no useful purpose, and are routinely extracted.

Little things matter. Proper adjustment of the curb strap or chain will ensure correct action of the bit. Too loose, and you lose control. Too tight, and the horse becomes uncomfortable and resistant. You should be able to place two fingers sideways between the chin groove and curb chain or strap.

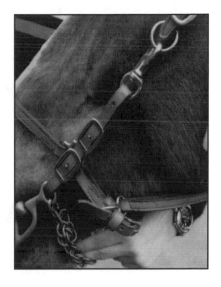

teeth. This can dramatically affect the way your horse responds to the bit. Most equine vets–and some lay practitioners–are experienced at teeth floating. If your horse dribbles grain, holds its head in a peculiar position while eating, or seems uncomfortable in the bridle–or if its droppings contain much undigested food–it should signal a call to your equine dentist. Make certain the person who performs the examination and work is tactful and experienced. Avoid those who depend on heavy metal devices to force and hold the horse's mouth open. In fact, ask directly if this is their practice. If it is, locate another person for the job. These devices are not only frightening to the horse, causing some animals to become head shy, but may be downright dangerous to bystanders.

When you're fitting the bridle, adjust it so that there is one wrinkle at each corner of the horse's mouth. Fit the curb chain or strap so you can easily place two fingers between it and the horse's chin groove when the bit is in the resting position. Any looser, and you'll lose the proper effect of the bit. Tighter, and you'll cause discomfort to the horse. This is especially important when riding in a bit with long shanks–the longer the shank, the more leverage on the curb chain. With your fingers between the curb chain and

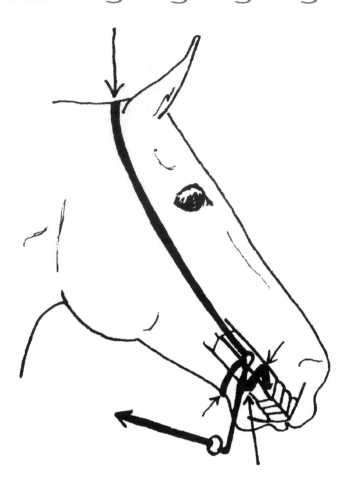

The actions of a curb bit are more complex than we might imagine. When the rein is pulled, the port in the mouth turns up so that there's pressure on the tongue and bars, as well as on the roof of the mouth. The chin strap or chain exerts pressure in the chin groove, and there's pressure at the poll besides. The longer the shanks, the thinner the mouthpiece, the tighter the curb strap, and the higher the port—the more severe the bit. It's important to understand how this device works so that we can use it for, rather than against, our horse.

the horse's chin, pull the shanks back to see how much pressure they cause the chain to exert.

In a curb bit, what happens when you pull on the reins is: the port rises up toward the roof of the horse's mouth, pressure is exerted on the tongue and bars, the curb chain presses into the groove under the horse's chin, and pressure is felt at the poll. Ideally, this action causes the horse to round out along the topline and poll and come onto the bit, tucking it's head into a position nearly vertical to the ground. To accomplish this, you need the mouthpiece, curb chain and shanks to be well balanced and operating together at maximum efficiency. If the bit is jointed at the corners, then there's additional action at the corners of the horse's mouth.

A horse with a short mouth may be more sensitive to the bit than one with a deeper mouth. Some horses with very deep mouths are able to work their tongue up over the bit. If this is the case, you may need to use a well-adjusted cavesson to keep the horse's mouth closed over the bit, or else use a bit with a deep port to hold the tongue in place. Some people use bits with 'rollers' in the mouthpiece. They claim this helps to relax a spirited, nervous horse. I sincerely can't say if this is a good idea or not, as I generally prefer a more laid-back type of mount. It does seem to me–and I've ob-

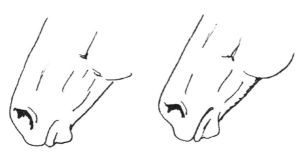

A horse with a shallow mouth (left) will be more sensitive to the action of the bit–and often easier to fit. A deep-mouthed horse may be able to work his tongue over the bit. Properly fitting such a horse may call for some ingenuity on the part of the owner!

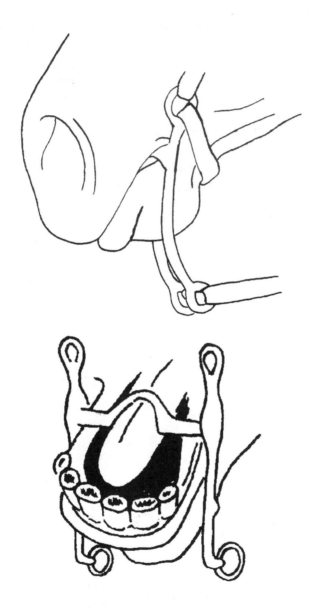

served this on several occasions–that these rollers tend to distract the horse. Rather than paying attention to the rider, he's playing with his bit. If you have a nervous horse and want to try a roller bit, by all means do so. It might be no more distracting to your horse than playing with a slinky toy is for us–uses up nervous energy, but doesn't prevent him from paying attention to business. If he uses it as an excuse to tune you out, try a different tactic.

If you do a lot of trail riding, I highly recommend a good grazing bit attached to a well-fitted leather halter/bridle combination. This will allow your horse to take a few snatches of grass on short rest stops without getting the grass all balled up around the bit. When you're ready for a more extended rest, you can slip the bit out of the horse's mouth and have a sturdy tie halter without going to the trouble of removing the entire bridle and replacing it with a halter. I prefer this to placing a bridle over the top of a halter, since a separate halter may interfere with the action of the bridle. I've seen people use the nylon halter/bridle combos, but they tend to stretch out over a day's ride. Since there's not much difference in price, go for the leather.

Being well-fitted for the trail means being prepared for any eventuality, and equipped to handle things as simply and efficiently as possible. This pair are the perfect example.

Shoeing

Ho boy! Here's a subject that is surely hot among gaited horse owners. Perhaps understandably so. Trimming and shoeing can make or break a gaited horse, and there's as much or more *mis*information out there as there is reliable information. I make no claim to be an expert on this subject. But I've made a study of it, and have figured out what principles seem to be sound, and which practices to avoid. Please don't rely primarily on this information, but seek the services of a farrier experienced with gaited horses.

First off, there's no substitute for basic sound shoeing practices. The shoe should precisely fit the foot from the toe, around the quarters, clear back to cover the heel. A poorly fitted shoe–particularly one that allows the horse's heel to hang over the back edge–will make for a miserable horse. Can you imagine wearing sandals that are too short for your foot? It wouldn't be long before you were hobbling along with sore heels. Same with your horse. You also want to make certain the shoe isn't too long, or your horse may step on the heel of the front shoe with the toe of his hind foot, causing it to tear right off, along with a chunk of foot.

The farrier should shape the shoe to fit the foot, rather than the other way around. The foot should be trimmed to an angle approximating the angles of the shoulder and pastern, with no more than a two or three degree variance to allow for gait improvement. Changes in foot angle should be made gradually, with no more than a one degree change at any one time. There–not *should*–but *must by law* (Horse Protection Act) be at least a one-inch difference between the length of the heel and the toe, with the toe of course being longer than the heel. To stand a horse more upright than this is inhumane and leads to certain lameness and breakdown. Though shoers of non-gaited stock tend to trim the foot very short, our gaited horses perform better with more hoof on the ground.

Here's what I've learned about angles. First of all, every horse is different. What is a high angle for one is only average for another. So no one should ever shoe a horse based on general information such as this–it all has to be planned according to the con-formation of the body, leg and foot of the individual horse.

On the whole, a 50° angle is considered about 'average.' A low angle–such as 45°–causes the horse to stand with a greater amount of angle between his foot and leg. The heel is low in relation to the toe. This is achieved with significantly different lengths between the heel and toe, with the toe being longer. If the toe is 5-1/2" long, and the heel only 3" long, you've got a low angle.

A high angle–such as 55°–means there is only a modest difference in length between the heel and toe, with both being cut relatively short, and the foot being more upright in relation to the horse's legs. This would be true if the toe were 4" long, and the heel 3" long.

Now let's say that a low angle is equivalent to wearing swim flippers, which places the foot at a greater angle to our leg, as a long toe, short heel does for the horse. How do you move with flippers on your feet? Do you not pick your feet up quite high and as soon as your foot is high enough to clear the toe, start setting the foot back down? Doesn't the longer 'toe' force you to take a much longer stride, and you land with greater weight on your heel? So you have a quick breakover with long stride. Your leg moves in a long, low, stretching arc. Same with your horse. A low angle encourage the horse to 'breakover' sooner–the breakover being the point at which the horse stops lifting and begins to arc his foot back toward the ground. It also encourages slower setdown for longer stride, or greater gait extension.

Let's take this one more step. In swim fins what happens to our other leg while one is moving forward? Does it not stay in position until the fore foot is firmly set on the ground? If forced to run in swim fins, would you not take long, low reaching strides, with no suspension? (Of course you might stumble–as might your horse, if the toe gets too long and unwieldy!)

A high angle works just the opposite. It might be equated to wearing high heels, which places our foot at *less* of an angle to our leg–short upright toe, high heel. This encourages a shorter stride but longer breakover point–you move your foot farther forward before starting to set it back down. Once you've achieved breakover, you set your foot directly down, with more weight on the toe. If a woman in high heels had to run quickly (Lord forbid!) she would be unable to take long, sweeping slow strides. She'd have to take shorter, faster steps to cover ground and keep her balance. There would also be a moment of suspension between footfalls as the trailing foot would pick up before the leading foot had quite set down.

Now let's see how changing the angles between the front and back feet of a gaited horse can help to encourage a particular gait. Let's first trim the foot with a low angle in front, and a high angle behind (flippers in front, high heels behind). In front we're encouraging the horse to move with a fast breaking, long reaching, non-suspensory stride. The hind legs have a slower breakover, a faster set-down after the breakover, a shorter overall reach, with suspension between footfalls. We've just described a pretty decent fox trot!

Now let's switch this around and trim for a high angle in front and a low angle behind (high heels in front, flippers behind). The horse will have slow breakover and shorter, faster stride in front, with some suspension between footfalls. There will be fast breakover with a slower, lower, longer reaching non-suspensory stride behind. Doesn't that sound like the ideal running walk?

Trimming and Shoeing To Correct Gait

Differing angles between the fore and hind feet encourage the horse to 'break up' a two-beat gait. Breakover and stride length between the fore and hind feet is altered, making it more difficult for them to move in exact synchrony, whether the horse tends to move laterally (pacey) or diagonally (trotty).

If your horse prefers a flat, two-beat pace–or a stepping pace–your farrier may help you square it up into a rack or running walk by increasing the angle of your horse's front feet (shorter toe, higher heel) and decreasing the angle behind (longer toe, shorter heel). This should be tried first with simple keg shoes of an appropriate size for the horse's foot. If this doesn't quite do the trick, try riding the horse either barefoot or with very light plates behind, and with

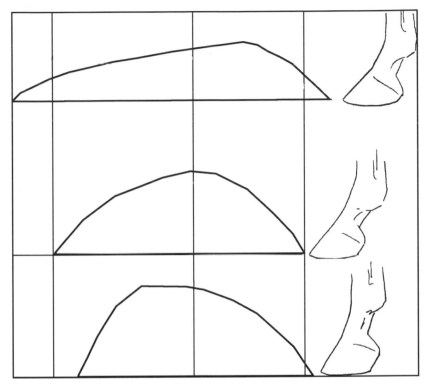

This graph illustrates the relationship to foot angle, breakover point and length of stride. The top foot is trimmed to a low angle, resulting in a fast breakover point and long, low reaching stride. The center foot depicts an average hoof angle, and the stride is average length and height with a breakover point about midway through it. The high angle of the bottom foot will cause a shorter, higher stride with a late breakover point.

a slightly heavier shoe in front. This will further (respectively) shorten/lengthen breakover.

I do not recommend going to what is commonly termed a 'plantation' shoe, as these are much too heavy for practical riding uses. The stress of carrying a too-heavy shoe will lead to long-term foot and leg damage. As you may have deduced, I also believe that pads, wedges, chains and every other kind of artificial gaiting device you can name should be avoided. Gait should be produced in the breeding shed, rather than in the metal shop.

For the horse that insists on trotting or fox trotting, the opposite tact may help the horse to move more laterally into a rack or running walk. Slightly decrease the angle of the front feet (longer toe, shorter heel), and increase the angle of the hind feet (short toe, high heel). If more alteration is necessary, shoe heavier behind and lighter in front.

Stumbling

If your horse is a stumbler, then I'm going to suggest a rather unique shoeing technique that might help. In fact, it's the opposite of what many people suggest–but I learned this method from a real shoeing expert. Besides, it makes sense!

Usually stumblers are shod with lighter shoes and/or shorter toes. Ask your farrier about shoeing the horse with a shoe one size larger than normal. Make certain the heels and quarters (sides) of the foot are well fitted, and leave 1/4" to ½" of shoe extended past the toe. The heavier shoe and longer toe will encourage the horse to pick up it's feet and put more effort into correct breakover. Since it will take the horse some time to get accustomed to this, let him wear the shoes a couple of days before riding him in them. Also, don't attempt any difficult terrain until he's learned to pick up those feet! After the horse has worn shoes like this for several weeks, he can go back to normal shoeing. Being forced to move correctly will have built up his muscles for doing so, and set him in the habit of picking up his feet.

Final Encouragement

Let me emphasize once again that nothing should *ever* be taken to extremes. A variance of three degrees from the horse's normal barefoot angle is a dramatic change–certainly the most that should ever be attempted. Even then the angle should only be changed about one degree at any given time. The goal is to obtain a good intermediate gait with as little change to the foot's natural angle as possible. If your farrier has to change your horse's foot angle two

degrees to change a trot to a fox trot, then content yourself with that gait rather than try for a squarer gait by altering the angle even more. If you're still not happy with the gait obtained using moderate trimming and shoeing methods, then concentrate on training methods–or get a different horse altogether.

Employing sensible, conservative methods may require several shoeings to meet your gait goals, so be patient. Nothing is gained by making the horse lame through overzealous alterations, and there's a great deal at risk. What benefit is obtained by rushing the job, if it makes your horse lame for several weeks, months– or forever?

Also keep in mind that your farrier is better qualified to make suggestions and changes than anyone else. He will be able to see how the horse moves, what condition the feet are in, the angles of the shoulder and pastern, etc. If your farrier happens to be totally unfamiliar with methods of shoeing gaited horses, then you have my permission to photocopy and share this section of chapter seven with him. If he thinks they make good sense, he can adapt the general principles to fit your particular situation. (Of course, female farriers are included in this as well!)

May you have many happy and smooth years–and trails!

Photo: Mickey Anderson

Chapter Eight
Corrective Exercise Routines

To encourage readers to actually get out and try the methods taught in this book, I've outlined some corrective training routines that will help to get you started on the right path. I'm convinced that if you will follow the appropriate plan outlined here, you'll see substantial improvement within six weeks. It's all right to work every-other day, but no less than that if you can possibly help it.

Routines for a Pacey Horse

To square up a pacey horse, take it through the following training routines. The entire time you're working with the horse, break up the exercises with cross country hacks where you do nothing more than walk, *walk, walk*. The more uphill work you can do on these walks, the better. Also don't be afraid to practice the exercises–keeping it casual–even while on the trail. It might seem like a lot of work, but I guarantee that you and your horse will learn to enjoy these sessions together, if you are diligent to keep at it. There is tremendous satisfaction in the work itself–and even more in the results!

179

Gaits of Gold

Week One

During the first week of work, keep it simple. Ask your horse to perform three or four neck bends to each side, and practice riding figure eights around cones for twenty or thirty minutes each day. While working the cones, concentrate on describing a perfect circle at each end, and upon perfecting your riding aids until you're using them without thinking.

Week Two

Do the same exercises in the second week of work as you did during week one, but begin to ask your horse for a little more speed around the cones. Do not allow her to break from the walk under any circumstances! Also practice the rein back and half-halts. By week's end the horse should be able to back up straight for several steps, and will noticeably respond to the half-halt.

Week Three

To the above routines, add neck stretching and *gentle* collection. If your horse will canter, add cantering to your circle work.

Week Four

During the fourth week you should be noticing a definite improvement in the horse's natural way of going and responses. Spend only a few minutes reinforcing what you've been working on during previous weeks. This week concentrate on asking for a bit more collection–don't overdo this. Since the horse can now stretch out along the topline, and collect, it should be able to handle a few stride lengthening and shortening exercises. These are tremendously beneficial, and once your horse knows what's expected, they can be used often when on the trail or in the arena.

If some of these routines seem to frustrate the horse, don't be afraid to backtrack and work at previous exercises a bit longer. You need to recognize and respond to your horse's capabilities, rather than stick to a rigid routine.

Week Five

It's time for some lateral work. Warm the horse up with a few of each of the above exercises. During the first part of the week, teach the shoulder-in. Once your horse is performing that well, work on haunches in. Five minutes to each side on each exercise is plenty, and will do a world of good.

Week Six

The horse can now stretch, bend, relax the topline, and respond instantly to your riding cues for any basic maneuver. Chances are she's already performing at least a decent amble, if not a rack or running walk. Performing some cavalletti exercises will help her to square up even more. As she gets the knack for this, ask for greater and greater speed.

Follow-up

Once your horse has been trained out of the pace, it's important to keep her in condition so that she doesn't get lazy and begin pacing again. This can be done with lots of trail and/or arena riding. Ask for frequent bending—whether you ask the horse to circle cones, or trees, doesn't matter. Also encourage your horse to stretch out along the topline, and then bring her back up into a nice rounded, collected frame. Use your aids to ask for shoulders and hauches in from time to time. Work her downhill and in deep going whenever you get the chance.

Routines for a Trotty Horse

During the time you're going through the routines below, ride your horse cross-country as often as possible. Downhill work is especially helpful—and you might use these opportunities to experiment with different bits. Bitting can be an extremely important consideration for a trotty horse.

Weeks One–Three

For the first three weeks, perform the same routines as outlined for the pacey horse. Get to know your new friend!

Week Four

Add stride lengthening and shortening exercises to your routine. Ask for greater and greater speed. If the horse breaks to a trot, try the 'swing' exercise to break it up. If this doesn't work, bring the horse back down to a walk, and continue asking for more collection, then extension, speed, etc. The idea is to get your horse lengthening and shortening both stride length and body frame at your cues.

Week Five

Practice collection, but allow the horse's nose to come up a bit more above the vertical. This will take some practice. Also start teaching your horse how to perform lateral exercises: shoulder-in and haunches in. As the horse is performing these maneuvers, ask for greater and greater speed during the course of the week. You might also work a spiral or two to each side each day.

Week Six

Concentrate on lateral work and lengthening and shortening stride. Continue to ask for more speed. Work the spiral exercise to each side several times each session—being sure to allow the horse to straighten out and go once or twice around the arena on occasion so that it doesn't tighten up and resist the intensive bending.

Follow-up

To keep the horse sharp once it's learned to move more laterally, exercise the horse regularly. **Never** allow it to flat trot. If it breaks to a trot, bring it back down to a walk and immediately ask for speed again. Don't reward your horse for trotting by bringing it back down to a lazy walk every time it breaks gait. Better to bring it back down, ask for speed, and go through a few lateral exercises at the same time. These should help to keep it from going back into a square trot.